Making & Keeping Friends

Ready-to-Use Lessons, Stories, and Activities for Building Relationships

Grades 4-8

Making & Keeping Friends

Ready-to-Use Lessons, Stories, and Activities for Building Relationships

Grades 4-8

John J. Schmidt, Ed.D.

JOSSEY-BASS
A Wiley Imprint
www.josseybass.com

Published by Jossey-Bass
A Wiley Imprint
989 Market Street, San Francisco, CA 94103-1741 www.josseybass.com

Jossey-Bass books and products are available through most bookstores. To contact Jossey-Bass directly call our Customer Care Department within the U.S. at 800-956-7739, outside the U.S. at 317-572-3986 or fax 317-572-4002.

Jossey-Bass also publishes its books in a variety of electronic formats. Some content that appears in print may not be available in electronic books.

Library of Congress Cataloging-in-Publication Data
Schmidt, John J.,
Making & keeping friends : ready-to-use lessons,stories, and activities for building relationships (grades 4-8) / John J. Schmidt.
p. cm.
ISBN 0-87628-553-1
ISBN 0-7879-6626-6 (layflat)
1. Friendship in children—Study and teaching—Activity programs. 2. Friendship in children—Study and teaching (Elementary) 3. Friendship in adolescence—Study and teaching—Activity programs. 4. Friendship in adolescence—study and teaching (Middle School)
I. Title.
BF723.F68S36 1997 97-16948
302.3'4'071—DC21

FIRST EDITION
PB Printing 10 9 8 7 6 5 4 3 2

DEDICATION

To students and colleagues
who have invited my friendship and enriched my life.

ACKNOWLEDGMENTS

There are many people to thank for helping me develop the ideas in this book. Dr. William W. Purkey has been my teacher, mentor, colleague, and friend for more than twenty years, and it is his development of "invitational theory" that provides the foundation for this book on friendship. The fifth-grade students, teachers, and counselors at H. B. Sugg and G. R. Whitfield elementary schools in Pitt County, NC, and the sixth-grade students, teachers, and counselors of Henderson County Schools, NC, who participated in pilot studies to test this curriculum in the classroom, were most helpful and offered many suggestions to improve the program. Christy W. Shields and Heather Robertson, two of my graduate assistants at East Carolina University, helped with research to strengthen the content of this book. I also must give credit to Dawn Bergquist, my daughter, who is now a teacher herself, for inspiring me to write the original book, *Invitation to Friendship* (1988), upon which this program is based. And most importantly, I thank Pat Schmidt, my wife and best friend, who always supports me in whatever project I undertake.

ABOUT THE AUTHOR

John J. Schmidt, Ed.D., is professor and chair of the Counselor and Adult Education Department at East Carolina University in Greenville, NC. He has been a social studies teacher, school counselor, director of counseling services, state coordinator of school counseling programs, and a university professor. In his career, Dr. Schmidt has worked with teachers and students at the elementary, middle, and high school levels.

Dr. Schmidt is an active writer and presenter in the field of counseling. He has authored or coauthored over 50 professional articles, manuals, and book chapters and 10 books, including *A Survival Guide for the Elementary/Middle School Counselor* (The Center for Applied Research in Education, 1991); *Counseling in Schools: Essential Services and Comprehensive Programs, 2d edition* (Allyn & Bacon, 1996); *Invitational Counseling: A Self-Concept Approach to Professional Practice* (Brooks/Cole, 1996); and *Living Intentionally and Making Life Happen*, revised edition (Brookcliff Publishers, 1994).

In 1979, Dr. Schmidt was named Elementary Counselor of the Year by the North Carolina School Counselor Association, and he has been awarded the Professional Writing and Research Award by the North Carolina Counseling Association on two occasions, 1988 and 1993. In 1997, that association presented him with its prestigious Ella Stephens Barrett Award for Leadership in the counseling profession. Dr. Schmidt is a National Certified Counselor, a Licensed Professional Counselor in North Carolina, and a member of Chi Sigma Iota, the international honor society in counseling.

ABOUT THIS PROGRAM

Making & Keeping Friends: Ready-to-Use Lessons, Stories, and Activities for Building Relationships (Grades 4-8) is a curriculum supplement for language arts, social studies, or other lessons. It is intended as a program for group discussion and classroom instruction about friendship and areas of student development related to the process of making and keeping friends.

Teachers, counselors, and other group leaders may want to have students read through this program aloud and discuss the different ideas found in each section. The program, including the activities in each section, is a useful resource for group discussion and classroom guidance lessons on friendship, conflict resolution, and self-development. In addition, the nine-section format fits well into a nine-week term.

This program is for young people who want to learn about themselves, about others, and about friendships. *Making & Keeping Friends* presents a specific process for developing meaningful and beneficial relationships with people. This specific process is called the "invitational model"; it was developed by Dr. William Watson Purkey and others, and presented in his book *Inviting School Success* (Purkey and Novak, 1996). His book is recommended for teachers and counselors who use the *Making & Keeping Friends* program. For a quick study of invitational theory, the Phi Delta Kappa "Fastback" #268, *Education: By Invitation Only*, provides an easy reference (Purkey and Novak, 1988).

Dr. William Purkey is a professor at The University of North Carolina-Greensboro, where he has spent many years teaching, studying, learning, and writing about the messages that people send to one another. One of his ideas is that people often send positive messages or do good things with one another. Dr. Purkey calls these actions "invitations," and he believes that when people send more invitations to themselves and to one another, their lives are enriched.

Throughout a lifetime, people form many friendships, which occur as a result of messages that they send to themselves and others. When they are successful with these friendly messages, other people respond by sending positive messages back to them. It is this process of sending and receiving beneficial messages that helps students make friends in their neighborhood, at school, and in other situations.

Sometimes the messages people send are helpful and strengthen their ties among friends. At other times, messages can be hurtful, and as a result they damage the friendships that people have made. Using this program, your students will learn about the messages they send to themselves and others, and how they can either help or hurt the friendships they are trying to build. The purpose of this program is to encourage students to select and send the most beneficial messages, so that they are seen by others as people with whom it would be advantageous to be a friend.

Making & Keeping Friends includes activities, stories, and role-play suggestions to reinforce the lessons. Students can do some activities by themselves, while others are best done in class or small groups. Teachers, counselors, and other group leaders are encouraged to read each section prior to the lesson, and to highlight parts of the section for students to read aloud in class. You may wish to reproduce each section as is or only selected parts for students to use. It is not recommended that this program be read in its entirety by students in class. Teachers and other group leaders should consider the reading level and other developmental aspects of their students in determining how much reading should be done by students.

This program teaches students how to form strong, lasting friendships by actively creating positive messages—"invitations"—to send to themselves and others. At the same time, the lessons ask students to examine negative messages they receive and send, and to learn how to handle these disinvitations in more positive ways.

The program consists of nine sections, each focusing on important ideas about making and keeping friendships. The first section explores friendship as an important part of everyone's life. In this section, students will read about the importance of friendship, factors that influence friendships, and characteristics that help make successful friendships.

Section 2 explores ideas about choosing friends and forming friendships. It also mentions ways to help students keep their friendships vibrant and healthy.

Section 3 defines *invitations* and shows students how they can use positive messages to develop long-lasting friendships. It also describes *disinvitations* and explains how these negative messages prevent friendships from developing, and sometimes destroy friendships that people already have. In this section, your students will also be introduced to *intentional* and *unintentional* behaviors.

Section 4 combines the elements of invitations, disinvitations, and intentions into four levels of functioning. Each level is important in understanding friendship. Also in this section, students will learn about *perceptions*, described as the ways that people "see" things. They will learn how people's perceptions influence friendships.

Section 5 describes how people use their perceptions to "see" themselves, and explains to students what we mean by a person's *self*. It illustrates how the *self* develops and how it changes during a person's lifetime. The exercises in this section will help students explore their own *selves*, thereby learning more about who they are. Self-knowledge is important because, as your students will learn, people must make friends with themselves before they are able to form friendships with others.

Section 6 of this program presents the steps for being an inviting friend. It also shares ideas about when to invite, why to invite, and whom to invite. These ideas make up the process of inviting oneself and others. The activities in this section help students learn ways to be successful in sending invitations to people with whom they want to be friends.

Section 7 discusses *when* to send an invitation and *when not* to send one. There are many choices that students make when inviting friendships, and sometimes one choice may be *not* to invite someone to be a friend. This section also discusses conflicts in friendships and, through activities and role play, asks students to examine behaviors that can help them resolve disagreements.

Section 8 asks students to examine their own behaviors. Desirable behaviors include acting appropriately, avoiding blame, and giving oneself positive instructions. In addition, this section encourages students to look at other behaviors that may help them become educated, celebrate life, and take time to do good things for themselves.

The last section combines the ideas found in the first eight sections and describes the importance of students' creating and sending themselves positive messages. Included in this section are ideas about knowing oneself, being healthy, staying healthy, and making friends.

Throughout this program, students will find "Gold Nuggets" that summarize important ideas about friendship and encourage them to establish alliances with new friends. Also, simple cartoons—"nebbishes"—emphasize particular ideas about friendships, self-understanding, and communication. You can use these nuggets and cartoons to stimulate group discussion about friendship, along with the activities that students can use to explore the world of friendship further.

Each section of this program begins with Group Leader Instructions. These instructions are for you—the teacher, counselor, or group leader—and they provide a summary of the objectives of each section, materials needed for each activity, a rationale for every activity, and instructions for each role play in the section. Vocabulary words that may be unfamiliar to students in grades 4-8 are also listed. The remaining text is intended for students to read.

John J. Schmidt

References

W. W. Purkey and J. M. Novak (1988). *Education: By Invitation Only*. Bloomington, IN: Phi Delta Kappa.

W. W. Purkey and J. M. Novak (1996). *Inviting School Success*. Belmont, CA: Wadsworth.

Note: For more information about invitational theory and practices, contact the International Alliance for Invitational Education, School of Education, The University of North Carolina at Greensboro, Greensboro, NC 27412-5001. Phone: (910) 334-3431; FAX: (910) 334-4120.

CONTENTS

Section 2
BECOMING FRIENDS

Section 3
LEARNING ABOUT INVITATIONS

Section 4
FOUR LEVELS OF ENCOURAGING OR DISCOURAGING FRIENDSHIP

Section 5
KNOWING YOUR SELF

Section 6
CREATING INVITATIONS TO FRIENDSHIP

Section 7
MAKING CHOICES AND RESOLVING DIFFERENCES

Section 8
CHOOSING POSITIVE BEHAVIORS

Section 9
SENDING YOURSELF INVITATIONS

APPENDICES

INTRODUCTION

GROUP LEADER INSTRUCTIONS

The Introduction can be read aloud in class, having students alternate the reading. You might find it appropriate to stop reading after a couple of paragraphs and ask students if they have any questions.

When students have finished reading the Introduction, ask them to write a definition of friendship. These definitions can be shared with the group and posted around the classroom. As various sections of the program are completed, students can refer to their definitions of friendship and compare the meanings with the lessons in the program.

Welcome to a program about friendship. This program is about how you can invite people to become your friends. More specifically, it is a guide to help you learn ways to make friends, now and throughout your lifetime.

This program is written for young people who want to learn about themselves, about others, and about friendships. *Making & Keeping Friends* presents a specific process for creating and developing relationships with people whom you want to call friends. It is also a program about communication.

Throughout your lifetime, you will form many friendships; they happen because of messages you send to yourself and to others. When you are successful with these friendly messages, people will respond by sending positive messages back to you. This process of sending and receiving positive messages will help you make friends with people in your neighborhood, at school, and in many other situations.

Sometimes the messages people send are very helpful and strengthen the ties among friends. At other times, messages can be hurtful and as a result, they damage the friendships people have made. In this program, you will learn about the messages that people send to themselves and others, and how they either help or hurt friendships. Its purpose is to help you select and send only the most beneficial messages, so that you are seen by others as a person with whom they would want to be best friends.

Some ideas in this program come from the work of Dr. William W. Purkey, a professor at The University of North Carolina-Greensboro. One of his ideas is that people often send positive messages or do good things with one another. Dr. Purkey calls these positive actions *invitations*, and he believes that when people send more invitations to themselves and to one another, their lives are much improved.

Making & Keeping Friends shows you how to form strong, lasting friendships by being more inviting toward yourself and others. It consists of nine sections, and each one focuses on important ideas about inviting friendships. Included in each section are stories, exercises, and activities that you can do by yourself, with your friends, or with other students to learn more about sending inviting messages.

Throughout this program you will find "Gold Nuggets" that summarize ideas about friendship and encourage you to establish alliances with new friends. Each section also contains activities that, with guidance from your teacher or counselor, you can use to explore the world of friendship. Some activities are starter suggestions to help you get to know yourself better. They also give ideas for forming lasting friendships with others.

I hope you enjoy this guide to friendship and find some ideas and "nuggets" for meeting new friends. Sometimes forming friendships is risky and a little scary; you might worry about what people will think of you. In *Making & Keeping Friends* you will learn that embarking on the journey toward friendship is well worth the risk. A life filled with friends is a life filled with enjoyment and fond memories. So invite a new friend today, and begin a wonderful adventure!

Dr. John J. (Jack) Schmidt

Section 1

UNDERSTANDING FRIENDSHIP

GROUP LEADER INSTRUCTIONS

Summary:

This first section introduces friendship by emphasizing the idea that students have control of their behavior and ultimately their decisions about the friendships they choose to make. The section begins with a story of two students who are new to Rockdale Middle School and how each student handles this "new" situation differently.

The section continues by exploring the importance of having friends, and introduces the concepts of sharing and helping in friendships. In addition, different kinds of friends are categorized as *social friends* and *best friends*.

The last part of this section considers the process of choosing friends, and examines factors that influence students' choice of friends. These factors include proximity, similarity, differences, and mutual affirmation.

Objectives

1. To introduce friendship and the concepts of "having friends," "sharing with others," and "helping others."
2. To define different types of friendships, such as "social friends" and "best friends."
3. To examine factors that influence the friendships people choose.
4. To examine personal characteristics that contribute to friendships.

Activities

Most of the time, students will be able to write their responses on the activity sheets. Some students may need more space, however, so you may want to give students lined paper as well.

Activity 1.1 follows the story of Rachel and Rocky, new students at Rockdale Middle School. The activity asks students to share their observations and opinions about various characters in the story. Activity 1.1 also asks students to identify characteristics of Rachel and Rocky with which they identify. The rationale is to have students think about and discuss traits and characteristics that may help them be successful in making friends.

Materials

- ❒ Story, "First Day at Rockdale"
- ❒ Copy of Activity 1.1 for each student
- ❒ Pencils or pens

Activities 1.2 and 1.3 ask students to think of a time when someone helped them with a problem and of a time when they helped someone else. Students should do these activities by themselves or with a partner, and then be invited to share in the larger group. *Caution*: Do not force a student to share if he or she resists. The rationale is for the group to identify feelings that people have when they are helped or when they help others, and to examine similarities and differences among these feelings.

Materials

- ❒ Copies of Activity 1.2 and Activity 1.3
- ❒ Pencils or pens

Activity 1.4 has students list the characteristics they look for in *social friends* and those they look for in *best friends*. The rationale is to begin identifying characteristics of friends and to compare differences about types of friends.

Materials

- ❒ Copies of Activity 1.4
- ❒ Pencils or pens

Activity 1.5 explores relationships that may have changed because friends have moved away. The rationale is to have students think about the effort it takes to keep "far away" friendships. Discussion can explore how similar effort is necessary to keep "nearby" friendships alive.

MATERIALS

- ❒ Copies of Activity 1.5
- ❒ Pencils or pens

Activity 1.6 examines the concept of *similarity* of traits among friends. The rationale is to encourage students to look closely at their likes and interests and compare this list with the likes and interests of their friends.

MATERIALS

- ❒ Copies of Activity 1.6
- ❒ Pens or pencils

Activity 1.7 asks students to explore the concept of *differences* among friends. The rationale is to promote acceptance of diversity and show how differences can enrich friendships as much as similarities.

MATERIALS

- ❒ Copies of Activity 1.7
- ❒ Pens or pencils

Activity 1.8 examines the word *affirmation* by asking students to use a dictionary to identify synonyms and related adjectives. The rationale is to expand the vocabulary students can use to describe beneficial friendships.

MATERIALS

- ❒ Copies of Activity 1.8
- ❒ Pens or pencils
- ❒ Dictionary

ROLE PLAYS

Each role-play activity throughout this program gives students the beginning of a script. In some instances, when the student players have completed acting out a written script, the class is asked to supply the ending for the role play. At other times, class members will be asked to observe what has taken place in the role play and comment on their observations. The object of these activities is to encourage students to learn new, more "inviting" expressions to help others and themselves form friendships.

In this first section, the role-play activities serve the following purposes:

Role Play 1-A. Encouraging someone who feels left out or is afraid of joining new groups.

Role Play 1-B. Affirming someone even though he or she has a negative attitude, thus taking an optimistic stance.

The Gold Nugget Metaphor

Throughout this and every other section of the program, students will have the opportunity to read "Gold Nugget" ideas. You may find it helpful to spend time introducing the concept of *metaphors* to students, and how metaphors are helpful in learning new ideas. One additional activity that may help students learn about metaphors is to think of other names for "Gold Nuggets." Two examples are: "Treasure Chest of Ideas," and "Sparkling Gems." See how many other names for these metaphors the students can create.

Vocabulary Words

The words below are found in this section and may need additional explanation by the teacher or group leader, depending on the reading level of students in the class. In addition, some of the words may convey *concepts* that need further explanation for students to comprehend. These words are identified with an asterisk (*).

enrich*
rehearse
fundamental
cherished*
conscious
circumstantial*
challenging
affirmation*
rhinoceros
characteristics
confide
coincidence*
harmonious*
proximity*
compile
synonyms

UNDERSTANDING FRIENDSHIP

The only way to have a friend is to be one.

Ralph Waldo Emerson

This program is about friendship. More specifically, it is a program to help you form friendships that enrich your life. It is about how people form friendships, the qualities contained in friendships, and why friendships are important. You will learn about a particular view of friendship—a view that will show you how to "invite" and build friendships for yourself with other people.

Before learning about this particular view of inviting friendship, you will first explore some ideas about friends and friendships. In this section, you will learn about choosing friends and about the factors that influence your choice of friends.

Before going further, read the following story about Rachel and Rocky, two new students at Rockdale Middle School. After you finish the story, answer the questions in Activity 1.1, and share your answers with your classmates.

FIRST DAY AT ROCKDALE

Rachel was excited about her first day at Rockdale Middle School. She was excited and a little scared. It is not easy leaving a school that you like and moving to a different school, particularly in November after the school year has already started.

Rachel was in the sixth grade and for the most part she liked school, except art classes. She never could draw or make things look the way they were supposed to. Once she made a clay horse and everyone laughed when Ricky Wallet said, "It looks like a rhinoceros!" Yet Rachel enjoyed her old school, and now riding the bus to Rockdale, she missed her friends—even Ricky.

During the bus ride, she thought about what it would be like getting off the bus and walking into her new school. She worried a little about what other students might say or do to her. Rachel thought about what her school counselor, Mrs. Watson, told her when they were saying good-bye her last day at Commerce School. Rachel confided that she was scared about going to a new school and Mrs. Watson said, "Think about all the good friends you have here at Commerce and when you get to Rockdale, look for people who remind you of us. When you see a student or teacher who reminds you of an old friend, walk up and say, 'Hi, my name is Rachel Hernandez and I'm new here. Can you help me find my way to class?'"

Mrs. Watson continued, "Sometimes making new friends is a little scary, but you can do it. Take charge, rehearse what you want to say, and if you are not successful the first time, try again. Soon someone will say, 'Yes. Welcome to our school! I can show you where your classroom is.'" Together, Rachel and Mrs. Watson practiced things to say when Rachel went to the new school.

On the bus, Rachel practiced silently as Mrs. Watson had taught her. Suddenly the bus stopped, and she looked out the window and saw the front of Rockdale School. The students on the bus began getting off and Rachel looked at their faces as they left. One girl caught her eye and Rachel smiled back at her. She followed the girl off the bus, caught up with her, and said, "Excuse me. My name is Rachel and I'm new here at Rockdale. Could you help me find my class?" The girl turned to her and said, "Hi, Rachel. I'm Barbara. I'm not sure where your class is, but that teacher over there is Mr. Jones, and he can help you. Come with me and I'll ask him for you."

That same morning, Rocky was also coming to Rockdale School for the first time. His mother was driving him to school because he missed the bus. Rocky wasn't pleased about coming to a new school and his mother was not happy that he had missed the bus. "Going to a new school will be good for you," she said. "Think of it as an adventure and you'll be fine." Rocky stared straight ahead and did not respond. His mother said, "You'll make friends. It will be great; you'll see. In any event, you might as well get used to it, because this is where we live now." As they pulled up to the front of the school, his mother reminded Rocky, "Remember, take bus 74 home. It will drop you right at the corner near our house. Don't forget—74."

Rocky stepped out of the car and watched his mother drive away. He stood on the sidewalk for a long time watching the other students as they hurried into the school building. At one point, a boy stopped, looked at Rocky, and said, "What's the matter? Are you okay?" Rocky mumbled, "I'm okay.

Leave me alone." The boy shrugged his shoulders and ran into the school. Rocky slowly walked toward the building and a bell rang. He heard a voice behind him say, "That's the last bell, son. You had better hurry up to class." Rocky turned and saw Mr. Jones, the teacher, standing in front of him. He looked down at the ground and mumbled, "I don't know where my classroom is." Mr. Jones replied, "Well, let me take you to the office and we'll find out which class you are in. What is your name?" Rocky answered softly. "Well, come with me, Rocky, and I'll help you find your room." As they walked into the school, Mr. Jones asked, "What bus do you ride?" Rocky mumbled, "I don't know."

Name ______________________________ Date ________________

ACTIVITY 1.1
Rachel and Rocky

Questions

1. Think about Rachel and Rocky on their first day at a new school. How did each of them handle this situation? Have you ever had a similar experience? How did you handle it?

2. Write down what you think about each of the other characters in this story.

   Mrs. Watson, the school counselor ______________________________

   ____

   Barbara, the girl on the bus ______________________________

   ____

   Mr. Jones, the teacher ______________________________

   ____

   The boy who asked Rocky, "What's the matter?" ______________________________

   ____

   Rocky's mother ______________________________

   ____

3. Who do you think would be most successful in making friends at the new school, Rachel or Rocky? Why do you think so? ______________________________

   ____

4. List the characteristics of Rachel and Rocky that you think are most like you.

   Rachel: ______________________________

   ____

   Rocky: ______________________________

   ____

HAVING FRIENDS

Most people want to have friends. It is part of being human. Throughout your life, you will have the opportunity to develop many friendships. Some of these may be brief, some may last many years, and a few might last a lifetime. People who enjoy themselves want to share that joy with others, and they want to help others enjoy their lives as well.

In the story, Rachel and Rocky both had the same opportunity to make friends at their new school. Unfortunately, Rocky did not "see" this opportunity in the same way that Rachel saw it. Later in this book, you will learn that the way people "see" a situation often influences how they handle it. Rachel made the effort to share her new experience with Barbara and that probably helped her make the new school all the more enjoyable.

Rocky resisted his mother's advice, as well as another boy's inquiry, and he was less than cooperative with Mr. Jones. All these behaviors are related to the way Rocky chose to look at his move to the new school. He was unwilling to share this adventure, and at the same time, he refused the help of others. He rejected two fundamental aspects of friendship: sharing one's enjoyment and helping others when they have a problem.

Role Play 1-A
"The Loner"

Instructions: Your group leader will choose two students to read each role, Rhonda and Billy, and then the class will write the final dialogue.

Rhonda: Billy, everyone has gone outside for free play. What are you doing in the classroom?

Billy: I don't want to go out; it's no fun out there.

Rhonda: You don't want to go out with your friends.

Billy: I don't have any friends.

Rhonda: ____

____

____

Sharing and Helping

It is human nature to want to be in the company of others. One reason that people want to have friends is that friendships make them feel wanted, and for most people this is a good feeling. It enriches our life when we share good feelings with others.

Another reason for having friends is that they can help you make decisions about what to do in certain situations. Sometimes people face difficult decisions in life, and the answers they choose can have lasting positive or negative effects. In these situations, friends can be supportive in helping you make difficult decisions.

Without friends to support you during difficult times, life might be very lonely. Having close friends to confide in when you have problems can be comforting. Similarly, having friends to share joyful events fills your life with cherished memories. Providing support and sharing joy are two reasons why people want to have friends. There are many other reasons why friendships are made, and because this is so, people tend to form several types of friendships with many different friends. In Activity 1.2, write your thoughts on support from friends. Activity 1.3 asks you to think about how you offered support to a friend.

Kinds of Friendships

Friendships occur in different ways depending on situations and circumstances. Sometimes friendships form quickly and are basically social in nature. Social friendships are more than acquaintances, yet they often do not reach deep levels of feeling. You have probably experienced many friendships like this in school, clubs, or your neighborhood. These friendships are marked by relationships that you characterize as "being friendly" or as "just friends." You like being with these people, you have fun together, you enjoy the same types of activities, and you consider them friends.

Other friendships in your life may have much deeper meaning. They are marked by strong feelings for another person that are demonstrated by caring, admiring, and sometimes even loving relationships. These types of relationships are characterized as "being close friends" or as "best of friends."

Perhaps you have already formed some of these types of friendships. If so, you can probably describe the differences between the friendships in which you are "just friends" and those with whom you are "best friends." You can use Activity 1.4 to write them down. Both types of friendships are very important in your life. You need friends to enjoy in a social way, but you also need close friendships that offer an opportunity for deeper personal meaning.

Understanding the importance of having social friends as well as the need to develop deeper friendships helps you to determine which friendships you want to choose. *Choosing* social friends is often the first step in developing deeper friendships.

Name ______________________________ Date ______________

ACTIVITY 1.2
Receiving Support

Think of a time when you were having difficulty. Answer the following questions and, if you feel comfortable, share your responses with a small group of students in your class. As you share your responses with each other, look for similarities and differences in the answers that each of you gives.

What was the difficulty? ______________________________

Did anyone help you with your problem? If so, who helped? ______________________________

Why do you think this person helped you? ______________________________

How did you feel when being helped by someone else? ______________________________

Name ______________________ Date ______________

ACTIVITY 1.3
Giving Support

Think of a time when you helped someone who was having difficulty. Answer the following questions and, if you feel comfortable, share your responses with a small group of students in your class. As you share with each other, look for similarities and differences in the answers each of you gives.

What difficulty was the person having? ______________________

How did you offer to help with the problem? ______________________

Why did you help? ______________________

How did you feel when helping someone else? ______________________

Name ______________________________ Date ______________

ACTIVITY 1.4
My Kind of Friends

Make two lists of five *characteristics* you look for in "social" friends and five that you want in your "best friends." Compare these two lists with each other and with the lists written by other students in your class. How similar is your "social friends" list with your "best friends" list? How similar are your lists with the lists of other students in your class? You can write some of your thoughts in the space provided.

My Social Friends Are:	**My Best Friends Are:**
______________________	______________________
______________________	______________________
______________________	______________________
______________________	______________________
______________________	______________________

Choosing Friends

Friendships usually do not happen by accident. You might meet people by accident, or by coincidence, but most of the time you form friendships on purpose. Return to the story of Rachel and Rocky. Rachel made a conscious effort to approach Barbara and introduce herself. If their meeting became a good friendship, we could say it was formed on purpose. Mr. Jones befriended Rocky, but it was mostly circumstantial because Rocky was dawdling before going into the school. If they became good friends, it would be because one of them made a purposeful effort to do so.

Most meaningful friendships are formed and developed purposefully, so it is important to think about how you choose your friends. Let us examine some of the factors that influence the choices we make regarding whom we want to be our friends.

Gold Nugget

Proximity

One obvious factor that influences friendship is *proximity*. This word means nearness to you. Most of the friends that you have chosen in your life have lived near you, gone to school with you, belonged to the same clubs as you, or attended the same place of worship as you. They have had close proximity with you. For many people, their "best friend" is often a brother or sister with whom they live!

Think about the friends you have right now. How many of your friends live in your neighborhood or apartment building? How many go to the same school with you, belong to the same clubs as you, or attend your church, synagogue or mosque? Do you have a friend who does not fit in any of the above categories? If so, it is likely that you met this friend through one of your other friends.

Of course, sometimes friends move away and you might still keep in touch with them even though they no longer attend your school, club, or place of worship. Do you have any friends like that? Nearness may have been a reason you chose them as friends, but other factors have now encouraged you to keep these friendships alive, even though they are far away. Those are good friendships to have. Use Activity 1.5 to write your thoughts on far away friends.

Similarity

Another factor that influences your choice of friends is *similarity*. Most people choose friends who have likes and dislikes that are similar to theirs. This is because friendships are usually built on harmonious relationships rather than on conflict. If two totally different people try to form a close friendship, it is possible that they will frequently disagree with one another. Frequent disagreements do not contribute to lasting friendships. Usually, people who look for close friends want to be with others who think and behave in ways similar to the ways they do.

Think of your friends. Do you like the same types of music, food, subjects in school, television shows, or other activities? Chances are that you probably have similar tastes, beliefs, and interests. If so, these factors have probably helped to establish your friendships.

Of course, it is good to have friends who are in some ways different from you. If everything about your friends were the same, life might get boring. Some variety and differences among friends add interest to relationships. They also challenge you to try new ideas and experiences. By sharing different ideas and challenging each other in acceptable ways, people show that their friendships have mutual benefit for themselves as well as for their friends. This belief in mutual benefit affirms each friend as a valuable and important person. Use Activities 1.6 and 1.7 to explore similarities and differences.

Name ______________________ Date ____________

ACTIVITY 1.5
Far Away Friends

Think about friends that you have who live far away. Write down their names and where they live. How did you become friends with them? How have you remained friends with such distance between you? Tell your classmates about a far away friend. And listen to them tell you about one of theirs. Write any additional thoughts in the space provided.

My Far Away Friends	Where We Met	How We Keep In Touch

Best Friends
Cartoon 1-A

Name ______________________________ Date ________________

ACTIVITY 1.6
Friendly Similarities

You have read the theory that most people choose friends who have similar likes, tastes, and interests as they do. Check this theory out by writing down in the left hand column your "likes and interests." Then list three of your friends and their interests. Compare the two lists and check how many likes and interests are the same. After you compile these lists, you might show them to your friends to see if they agree with the interests and likes you listed for them. Use the space below for additional thoughts.

My Likes and Interests	Friends' Names	Their Likes and Interests
____________	(1)____________	____________
____________	(2)____________	____________
____________	(3)____________	____________
____________	(1)____________	____________
____________	(2)____________	____________
____________	(3)____________	____________
____________	(1)____________	____________
____________	(2)____________	____________
____________	(3)____________	____________

Name ______________________________ Date ______________

ACTIVITY 1.7
Experiences of Differences

Sometimes differences among friends help to enrich their relationship. Write down some of the differences between you and one of your friends. How do these differences help your friendship?

I am: ______________________________

My friend is: ______________________________

I: ______________________________

My friend: ______________________________

I like: ______________________________

My friend likes: ______________________________

Affirmation

Another factor that influences your choice of friends is *affirmation*. Affirmation means that people treat you as a valuable and worthwhile person, and you treat them in similar ways. Often, people seek friendships to give their lives meaning and to help them achieve a feeling of importance. Good friends contribute to this process of affirmation.

You probably do not associate with people who treat you with disrespect, who ignore your opinions, or who put you down when you are around others. By the same token, your friends want to know that you believe they are valuable and worthwhile people too. They want you to show respect toward them by listening to their point of view, keeping secrets they share with you, being honest with them, and treating them kindly when you are with other people. Write your ideas on affirmation in Activity 1.8.

Role Play 1-B
Anita's Problem

Instructions: Your group leader will ask three students to take the roles of Anita, Babs, and Shaquita (or Robert, Jeremia, and Ted). The three students will meet before the role play and write the ending. After the role play, the class can think of other possible endings.

Anita: Babs, let's go to your house and play "Hawk's Revenge" on your computer.

Babs: But I just asked Shaquita to come home with me. We were going to do math homework together.

Anita: Shaquita! Why would you want to ask her? She's a "know-it-all."

Babs: Well, I like being with her.... Quiet, here she comes.

Shaquita: Hi, Anita! Are you ready to go, Babs?

Babs: Yes, but Anita wanted to come and play a game on the computer.

Anita: No, I don't want to go. You two can go do your stupid homework.

Shaquita: ____

____

____

Name ______________________________ Date ______________

ACTIVITY 1.8

Affirmation Synonyms

Look up the word *affirmation* in a dictionary and write down synonyms that relate to how affirmation applies to friendship. After you have a list of synonyms, translate them into adjectives that you think relate to friendship. For example, one synonym of affirmation is *approval.* If we change this to an adjective it becomes *approved.* Do you think the friends you have should be *approved* by others such as your family and other friends? Use the extra space to write your thoughts.

Affirmation Synonyms	Related Adjectives
______________________________	______________________________
______________________________	______________________________
______________________________	______________________________
______________________________	______________________________

Factors such as proximity, similarity, and affirmation help you to select people whom you want as your friends. At the same time, diversity and differences can stimulate and enrich your friendship. Once you make the decision about whom you want to be your friend, the next step is to begin forming the friendship. In the second section, we will consider this process of forming friendships.

Section 2

BECOMING FRIENDS

GROUP LEADER INSTRUCTIONS

Summary:

Section 2 continues the discussion of friendship by introducing steps that students may use to make and keep friendships. In forming friendships, students learn about "breaking the ice," being optimistic, showing respect, and developing trust. Keeping friendships intact requires caring behaviors and methods of evaluating one's friendships.

This Section also introduces the concept of *intention,* and relates it to four types of friends:

—Friends who wait for things to happen
—Friends who wonder what happened
—Friends who always watch things happen
—Friends who make things happen.

Friends who make things happen, rather than simply waiting, watching or wondering, are those who behave with the most "intention." The concept of intention is important to the whole idea of inviting and making friends, as students will see in Sections 3 and 4.

Objectives

1. To learn steps that one can take in making and keeping new friends.
2. To examine characteristics, qualities, and behaviors that are important in forming and evaluating friendships.

ACTIVITIES

Activity 2.1 asks students to remember a time when they were asked to do something new, and to recall their feelings about this new venture. The challenge of forming new friendships may bring on similar feelings that students may want to discuss. The rationale is to have students explore feelings related to making new friends and learn that these are normal feelings shared by many of their classmates.

MATERIALS

- ❒ Copies of Activity 2.1.
- ❒ Pencils or pens
- ❒ Chart paper or chalkboard for large group sharing

Activity 2.2 is an enjoyable activity that asks students to create pessimistic thoughts and phrases that might jeopardize an otherwise optimistic friendship. The rationale is to explore the negative *self-talk* people sometimes use, and to see the absurdity in pessimistic thoughts.

MATERIALS

- ❒ Copies of Activity 2.2
- ❒ Examples written out on chart paper or the chalkboard
- ❒ Pencils or pens

Activity 2.3 asks students to write a *helpful* letter to Bossy Philip. The activity can be done individually by students, in pairs, or in groups. The rationale is to help students learn constructive ways to help their friends examine behaviors that interfere with relationships.

MATERIALS

- ❒ Copies of the story Bossy Philip
- ❒ Copies of Activity 2.3
- ❒ Pencils or pens

Activity 2.4 challenges students to find all the words related to trust in the word puzzle. Students are then asked to write antonyms for each of the trust words they find. The rationale is to build students' vocabulary. *(Answers to Activity 2.4:* believable, faithful, reliable, certainty, dependable, assurance, confidence, responsible, commitment, hope.)

MATERIALS

- ❒ Copies of Activity 2.4
- ❒ Pencils or pens

Activity 2.5 asks students to examine the difference between making excuses and taking responsibility for one's behavior. Students are instructed to think of behaviors that sometimes get them in trouble with others. They are then asked to write down common excuses they sometimes use to explain these behaviors.

After listing all the excuses, students write down new phrases that demonstrate more self-responsibility. The rationale is to have students examine some thoughts and behaviors that keep them from being self-responsible.

MATERIALS

- ❒ Copies of Activity 2.5
- ❒ Pens or pencils

Activity 2.6 instructs students to write down five behaviors that might jeopardize their friendships. Next to each behavior they write a response they would use if one of their friends behaved this way. The rationale is to have students explore their own behaviors and reflect on how they might change.

MATERIALS

- ❒ Copies of Activity 2.6
- ❒ Pens or pencils

Activity 2.7 asks students to brainstorm different topics of interest—things they like to do, school subjects they enjoy, and so on. When you have a list of five or more topics, write them on the top of separate pieces of newsprint. Place the newsprint around the room and ask the class to walk around and sign up for interest groups by writing their names on *one* or *two* of the lists. When everyone has signed a list, share them with the class and lead a discussion about these common interests.

MATERIALS

- ❒ Copies of Activity 2.7
- ❒ Chalkboard
- ❒ Newsprint
- ❒ Markers or pens

Role plays

Role Play 2-A. Approaching someone new to your school.

This role-play activity gives the beginning of a script. Student 1 must supply a dialogue when meeting the new student. The class might suggest the closing response for the new student. Additional dialogue among the three students can be created.

Vocabulary Words

These words may need additional explanation by the group leader, depending on the reading level of students in the class. Words with an asterisk denote concepts that may need explanation.

fortified
interactive*
complex*
optimism/optimistic
nonjudgmental*
pessimism/pessimistic
circumstances
jeopardize
monopolize

ingredients
miscommunication*
unreliable
reliance
compromise*
eliminating
evaluating
intention*
threatened

BECOMING FRIENDS

Life is to be fortified by many friendships.
To love, and to be loved, is the greatest happiness.

Sydney Smith

In the first section of this program, you learned about friendships and the qualities that help people decide whether to become friends. This second section explores steps you can take in forming new friendships.

FORMING FRIENDSHIPS

Choosing whom you want as friends is relatively easy. Taking steps to form friendships is more difficult because forming friendships can be risky. It is one thing to choose a person to be your friend, but it is quite another for that person to choose you as well. Because this is so, it is helpful to understand what goes on when people try to make new friends. One way to understand this interactive process we call "making friends" is to examine your feelings as you begin to form new relationships.

Breaking the Ice

Think for a moment of one of your best friends. Can you remember when the two of you first met, and how you felt as you began to form a friendship? If you are like most people, you probably felt a little unsure, and maybe even a little scared. A good illustration of this feeling of uncertainty and nervousness is to think about a time a teacher wanted you to try something new in class. Maybe it was a new math problem, a complex computer program, or a challenging athletic skill. If you remember such an incident, you probably can recall your feelings about approaching this new venture. You can explore these feelings further in Activity 2.1.

Name ______________________________ Date ________________

ACTIVITY 2.1
An Anxious Adventure

Think of a time that someone asked you to do something new. It may have been a request of a teacher, brother, sister, or friend. Try to remember an occasion when you were invited to do something you had never tried before. As you recall this event, write down the feelings you remember as you began this new venture. After you list the feelings you remember, share the event with a classmate and talk about the feelings you listed. Ask your classmate to share his or her event and the corresponding feelings with you, and compare your experiences.

The event was: ____

____

My feelings were: ____

____

____

____

____

____

____

____

____

____

____

____

____

____

____

____

____

____

____

____

____

Gold Nugget

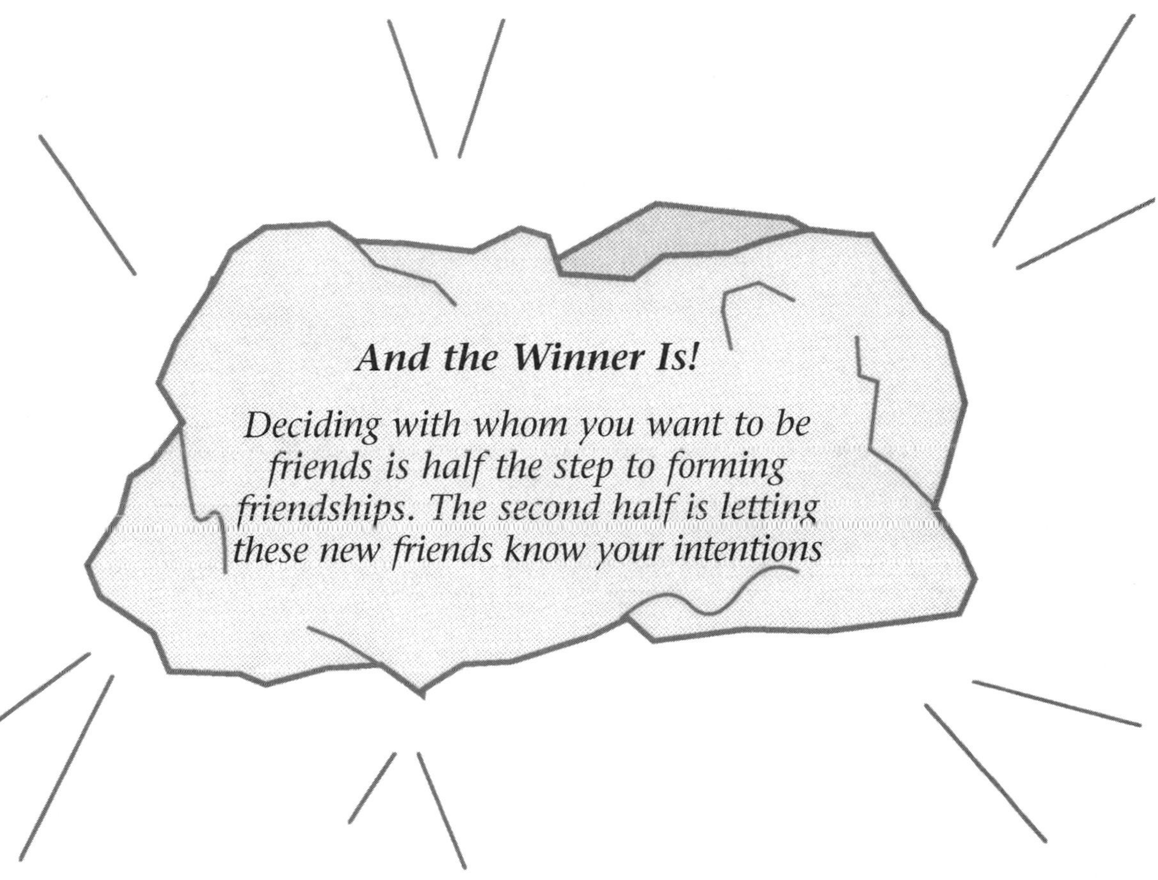

Another example of feelings that occur in new situations is when young children meet each other for the first time. Some young children who have never met before often approach each other very carefully. They may not look at each other, but rather glance out of the corners of their eyes. They do not talk right away, and they carefully look each other over, while watching the other's behavior. Then, if they decide to approach, they do so ever so slowly. As they become more comfortable with each other, they begin to talk and play, enjoying their time together.

Young children meet the way some people go into a swimming pool. Unlike swimmers who immediately dive into the pool head first, some less brave souls are more cautious. First, they put one big toe in, then a foot, and slowly they walk into the pool up to their waists. When they feel the water is "just right," they dive all the way in!

Older children and adults are also cautious when they approach strangers, but they are probably more verbal and formal in their introductions. For example, a girl might introduce herself by saying, "Hi, I'm Janet. Do you go to school here?" These behaviors, whether by young children or adults, serve the purpose of "breaking the ice" and getting acquainted with other people. One key to being successful in these early "ice breaking" relationships appears to be an element of *optimism*. The first step in forming successful friendships is establishing your own positive attitudes—in other words, being optimistic.

Being Optimistic

Optimism means believing that good things are going to happen. Optimistic people are able to form successful friendships because they believe in themselves and in their ability to get along with others. They also have positive views about other people. No matter what other people look like or act like, optimists think positively about them; while they are cautious about approaching strangers for purposes of safety, they remain pleasant and nonjudgmental about most people they meet.

Being optimistic makes much more sense than being pessimistic, which is the opposite. What would you think if a student you did not know approached you and said, "Hello. You don't know me and probably don't want to, but I'd like to be your friend"? How different would you feel if instead the same student said, "Hello. You don't know me, but I've noticed you at school and would like to get to know you better"? You can make up your own pessimistic approaches in Activity 2.2.

Optimistic relationships examine the possibilities of what *can* be, rather than what can't be. From the initial feeling of uncertainty that people have when approaching new friends, they eventually feel more comfortable as these new relationships continue. They will feel more and more comfortable as long as their friendships continue in hopeful, optimistic directions.

Too often, friendships falter because people allow their own fears to prevent them from accepting new challenges. Such people are often heard using the phrase "I can't." Optimistic friendships avoid the *can'ts* by spending energy on what *can be done*. This does not mean that optimistic friends force their will on others. To the contrary, it means that optimistic friends expect their relationships to have a positive, forward direction, while at the same time respecting the views of others. Having respect for others is the next step in the process of forming successful friendships.

Name ______________________________ Date ______________

ACTIVITY 2.2
Pessimistic Frolic

Just for fun, think of pessimistic thoughts and words that people might choose in attempting to form friendships. Make up some humorous ones and share them with your classmates. Here are some samples to get you started:

> "You can play, but not too hard because I might fall down and get hurt."
> "I'm not very good, but may I be on your team?"
> "Let me go to the mall with you, but don't walk too fast; I get tired quickly."

Role Play 2-A
New Student

Instructions: Your group leader will choose three students to read each role, then, the class will write the final dialogue.

Student 1: Hey, who's that over there?

Student 2: Oh, that's (name), a new student—came yesterday.

Student 1: Let's go talk to (him/her).

Student 2: Naw, I don't want to.

Student 1: C'mon. (Student 1 walks over to new student and student 2 follows).

Student 2: ____

____

____

____

New Student: ____

____

____

Having Respect

Becoming comfortable with people means that you are able to share mutual respect with them. Mutual respect is established when people show that they care for each other's feelings, opinions, and desires. The opposite is *disrespect* for others. People are disrespectful when they do not care about what others want, or how they feel. Disrespect is a major barrier to friendship, and it causes problems in other relationships as well. An example of why this is so can be seen in the story of Philip.

BOSSY PHILIP

Philip was a new boy in the neighborhood and he wanted very much to make friends with other children. Most of the children in the neighborhood were friendly toward him and frequently asked Philip to join them in games

> and other activities. But Philip had a problem. When he participated in games or other events, he had this strong urge to be in charge—to be the "boss." As a result, he would often make up his own rules and take control of the game or activity. As you can imagine, the other children disliked this. They wanted their ideas and wishes respected, but Philip was like a powerful locomotive running full steam ahead. In time, the other boys and girls in the neighborhood gradually stopped inviting him to join them.
>
> This, of course, hurt his feelings, but instead of trying to see how he could change his own behavior, Philip tried to "get even" by being mean and even more disrespectful toward the others. This did not improve things, and Philip continued to lose friends.

Use Activity 2.3 to think of ideas about how you might help someone like Philip. By identifying behaviors that help other people make friends, you expand your own friendship behaviors.

Showing respect for others, as you have done in the letter to Philip, is not hard, but it does take effort. Even under the most trying circumstances with the most difficult people, you can still be respectful. By being consistently respectful toward others, you gain their respect as well.

Gaining the respect of other people takes initiative and responsibility. You work at gaining respect by being respectful toward those around you, including people who are not necessarily your friends. You respect their feelings by being kind to them, you respect their belongings by asking permission to borrow things, and you respect their freedom by not forcing them to accept all your wishes. It is through these respectful behaviors that you are able to move your friendships further along by developing *trust* in one another.

Developing Trust

As friendships continue to develop, mutual respect among friends becomes greater because they *trust* each other. Trust is the ability to have faith in another person. It means having faith that the other person will treat you kindly and will not harm you. By the same token, the other person has similar feelings about you, and these mutual feelings help your friendship grow stronger.

While trust develops friendships, its opposite, *distrust*, destroys them. Earlier in this section, you learned that friendships develop when people become more comfortable and show faith in one another. If that faith is broken, friendships can end immediately. Sometimes, trust takes a long time to win, but it can be lost in a split second. Perhaps you have had friendships that ended because trust was broken. There are many ways this can happen. For example, sometimes it happens because a friend tells a secret that you were keeping. If a friend reveals secrets to others, trust may be shattered beyond repair.

Sometimes trust is jeopardized simply because of miscommunication. Someone says something and as the message goes forth and gets repeated, it becomes confused

Name ______________________________ Date ________________

ACTIVITY 2.3
Helping Philip

In the story about Philip, the other children seemed willing to have him participate, but his bossiness turned them away. If you knew Philip, how could you try to help him? Are there optimistic and respectful things you could do or say that might help him? Think about what you might say to Philip, and write a letter to let him know you want to be his friend.

Dear Philip,

____

____

____

____

____

____

____

____

____

____

____

____

____

____

____

____

____

____

____

____

____

____

Sincerely,

and mistaken. At other times, people may send us a message, like an invitation to a party, but it gets lost and we never receive it. Even though these miscommunications and lost messages are not done on purpose, they sometimes cause us pain and difficulty in our relationships.

Another way that trust is weakened and sometimes broken occurs when people are unreliable or not dependable. Friendships are formed because people want to *rely* and *depend* on others. When reliance and dependence no longer exist, there can be little trust. An example of this is when friends constantly use excuses or blame others for their own behaviors and mistakes. Find the words related to trust in Activity 2.4.

Suppose you have a friend who is usually late and keeps you waiting, but always has an excuse or blames someone else for being tardy. If your friend continues to behave this way, you will probably tire of the relationship. You will no longer believe the excuses, which means that you will no longer trust this friend. When you form

Gold Nugget

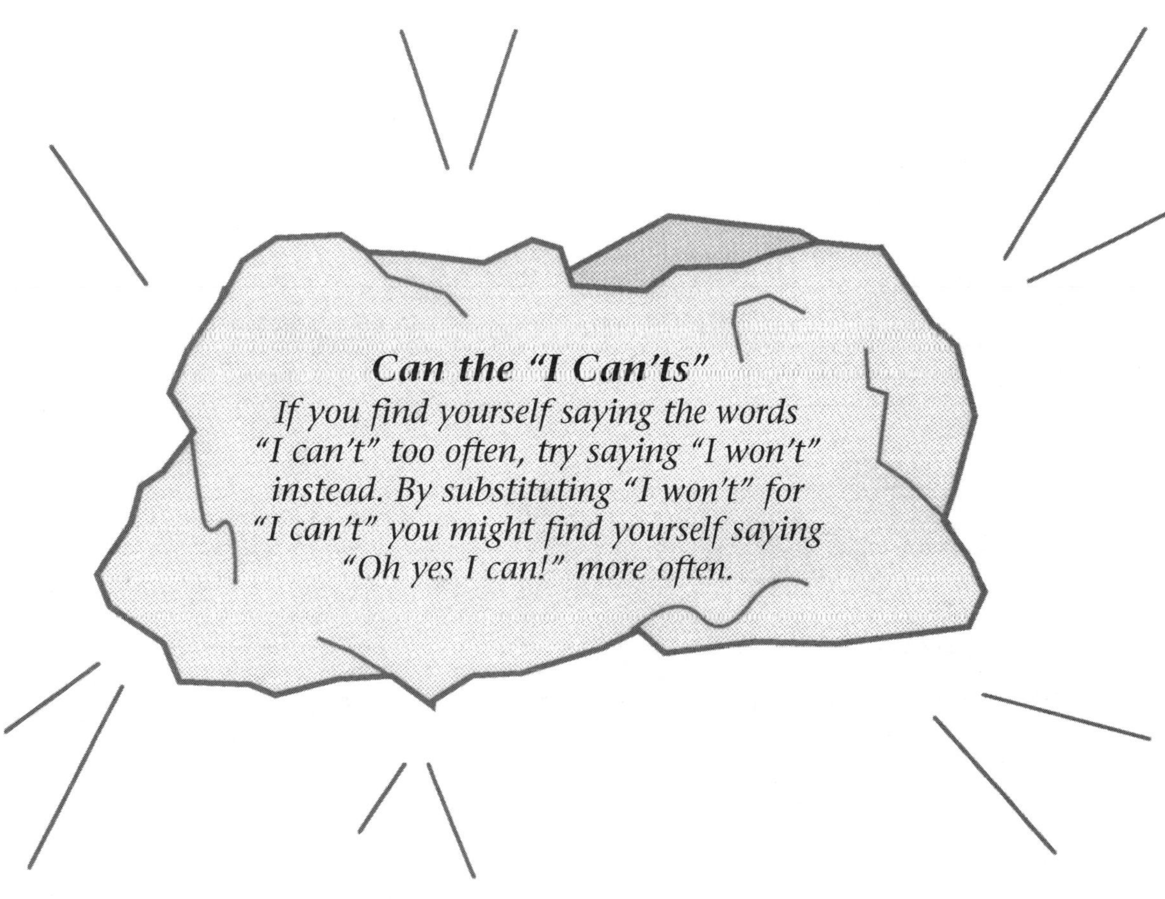

Name ______________________________ Date ________________

ACTIVITY 2.4
Finding Trust

Locate all the words that are related to trust in the word puzzle. Some are written backwards and some from top to bottom or bottom to top. Write the words in the Trust list (a total of 10 words), and then write the opposite of each word, an antonym, in the Distrust list. (Your group leader has the answers.)

a	l	e	l	b	a	v	e	i	l	e	b	e	f	c
o	u	f	j	e	s	h	l	p	j	l	x	c	t	o
b	f	f	c	l	s	f	b	p	k	b	v	n	z	m
p	h	o	e	b	u	t	a	a	v	i	j	e	k	m
a	t	m	r	a	r	i	d	b	z	s	l	d	l	i
s	i	w	t	i	a	s	n	q	h	n	k	i	t	t
y	a	x	a	l	n	o	e	k	z	o	o	f	o	m
d	f	t	i	e	c	q	p	r	q	p	p	n	j	e
z	z	e	n	r	e	v	e	q	x	s	h	o	e	n
o	x	r	t	q	n	u	d	r	n	e	w	c	d	t
r	m	j	y	k	h	o	p	e	t	r	a	w	z	x

Trust List

____
____
____
____
____
____
____
____
____
____

Distrust List

____
____
____
____
____
____
____
____
____
____

Name ______________________________ Date ______________

ACTIVITY 2.5
Excuses, Excuses

Think of behaviors that sometimes get you in trouble with your parents, teachers, or friends. List the behaviors in the left column. After you have listed at least three behaviors, write down the excuses you sometimes use for these troubling behaviors in the middle column. When you have listed all your excuses, use the right hand column to rephrase your excuses so that you take more responsibility for your behavior, using the pronoun "I."

Problem Behavior	**Excuses**	**Taking Responsibility**
Example: Fighting with other students.	They make me mad.	I lose control of myself.

deep friendships, trust cannot be compromised. You must consistently work at developing trust in these meaningful relationships.

As seen in Activity 2.5, the difference between making excuses and taking responsibility is often the difference between using the pronoun "they" and using the pronoun "I." When we begin statements with "they," we tend to blame others for our misbehaviors. On the other hand, if we begin by saying "I," we have a good start on assuming responsibility for our actions. Being responsible and eliminating excuses is one way of establishing trustful relationships.

Trust, like optimism and respect, is an important quality in friendships. As you will see, these three qualities are also important in becoming an "inviting" friend. You will learn more about optimism, respect, and trust in Section 3 of this program.

All three of these qualities combine to create the *courage* needed to form friendships. Friendships do not always come easily. You have to be willing to take the risk that sometimes people will not accept your friendship right away. When people reject your friendship, it may hurt, but if you never take the risk to make friends, you may never know the joy of these relationships. If you have the courage and maintain it, some of your friendships will last a lifetime.

Keeping Friendships

The qualities required when choosing friends and forming new relationships are also found in lasting friendships. Optimism, trust, and respect must be kept at high levels for relationships to last a long time. When one or more of these ingredients are weakened or neglected, friendships break up.

As you have already seen, most friendships do not happen by accident. They are carefully developed and nurtured over time. For friendships to continue, they must be kept in good working order. This means that friends must remain optimistic, continue to win the respect of others, and behave in trustworthy ways. Developing these qualities to keep friendships alive requires specific action that shows how you *care* for others and *evaluate* your relationships.

Caring

Much like tending a flower garden, keeping friendships requires action that results in a harvest of positive relationships. Just as flowers need water, sunlight, food, and care, friendships require similar attention. A well-tended garden will produce flowers in much the same way that friendships produce a lifetime of enjoyment and pleasure. On the other hand, an untended garden will not produce healthy, beautiful flowers any more than a neglected friendship will result in a positive relationship.

Developing positive friendships requires actions that have specific direction and purpose. In other words, if you are going to care about your friendships, you have to have good *intentions*. Good things sometimes happen by luck or accident, but if you really want strong friendships, you have to *make* good things happen.

One way to think about friendships and intentions is to consider that there are basically four types of friends. The first type is a friend who *waits for good things to happen*. This is a person who does not actively participate in a friendship. Instead, he or she sits back and waits for others to take action. For example, some people almost never ask others to join them in an activity; they simply wait for others to invite them.

A second type of friend is one who *wonders what happened*. This person never takes responsibility in a friendship, and usually blames others when things go wrong. It is as if bombs are always exploding around this type of person, and he or she wonders, "What else could possibly happen to me?"

The third type of friend is one who *watches things happen*. These friends are spectators. They sit on the sidelines and rarely join in the fun. They enjoy watching, but seldom participate.

It is the fourth type of friend who becomes involved and *makes things happen*. These friends actively participate in their relationships by intentionally planning and doing things to show that they care about others.

The root meaning of the word *intend* is "to tend" or, in other words, "to care" for something. As you have seen, it is important "to tend" to your friendships in much the same way that you might "tend to" your garden. Intention is an important quality in friendships, and one that you will learn more about later in this program.

Because caring requires direction and purpose, it is necessary to determine *which* direction and *what* purpose. In friendships, it is important to know where you are headed, and why you are going there. To know this, you want to consistently evaluate your friendships.

Evaluating

Evaluating friendships means asking yourself about your friends, your relationships with them, and what they mean to you. Returning to the illustration of the flower garden, you can see that similar evaluation takes place.

When flowers are picked each season, the gardener determines how nice they look and whether or not the same kinds of flowers should be planted again. Different species of flowers grow successfully, depending on the location of the garden, the amount of sunlight received, and the quality of the soil. Also, the kinds of flowers that are grown will depend on the preferences and needs of the gardener.

Friendships are similarly evaluated. You want friendships that will help you feel wanted, valuable, and important. Friendships that satisfy these feelings are tended to like a garden. Those that do not are either neglected or broken.

Sometimes people neglect friendships, not because their needs are unsatisfied, but because they forget that friendships require commitment and attention. When this happens, friendships frequently end, and people wonder why. An example of this is the story of Stephania, a girl who made friends easily.

Loves Me, Loves Me Not
Cartoon 2-A

NO RETURN STEPHANIA

Stephania had many friends, but not many close friends or longtime friends. It seemed that she liked it when others invited her to join their activities and shared things, but Stephania seldom returned the favor by reaching out to others. As a result, her friends soon got tired of always doing the inviting and sharing, and they moved on to other friendships. Stephania did not realize that friendships are partnerships that require both parties to contribute to the relationship. Because Stephania did not participate equally in her friendships, her friends felt their relationships were one-sided. These kinds of friendships seldom last long.

On occasion, friendships must be evaluated for the harm they may be doing. Sometimes people get into relationships that are harmful instead of helpful. For example, if a friend asked you to steal something, what would you do? Stealing is wrong. It is not a helpful action and persons who call themselves "friends" and encourage you to steal must be reminded that your friendship is based on optimism, trust, and respect. Stealing does not fit with any of these qualities, because true friendships are equally helpful to everyone involved. Examine friendship behaviors in Activity 2.6.

Another example of a friendship that needs to be evaluated is when a friend constantly questions your loyalty because of other friendships you have made. Friends who try to monopolize your friendship and prevent you from forming other relationships must be questioned. True friends welcome the opportunity to expand their friendships and are not threatened by your desire to have more friends.

Keeping friendships, as you have seen, requires specific behaviors that focus on the continued development of optimism, trust, and respect, and on the evaluation of the benefits of each relationship. Choosing, forming, and keeping friends all require behaviors that are optimistic, trustworthy, and respectful. The development of such behaviors needs a specific plan of action. Beginning with Section 3 of this program, you will learn about a specific plan called "inviting friendships." To prepare for these invitations, use Activity 2.7.

Name ________________________________ Date ________________

ACTIVITY 2.6
Evaluating Friendships

Think of behaviors that you believe might jeopardize your friendships. Write down five behaviors in the left-hand column. Think of ways you would choose to respond to each of the behaviors. What would you do or say if a friend of yours behaved this way? Write your thoughts in the space provided.

Behavior	**Your Response**
______________________________	______________________________
______________________________	______________________________
______________________________	______________________________
______________________________	______________________________
______________________________	______________________________
______________________________	______________________________
______________________________	______________________________
______________________________	______________________________
______________________________	______________________________
______________________________	______________________________
______________________________	______________________________
______________________________	______________________________
______________________________	______________________________
______________________________	______________________________
______________________________	______________________________
______________________________	______________________________
______________________________	______________________________
______________________________	______________________________
______________________________	______________________________
______________________________	______________________________
______________________________	______________________________
______________________________	______________________________

Name ______________________________ Date ______________

ACTIVITY 2.7
Who's on Your List?

Brainstorm different topics of interest—things you like to do, school subjects you enjoy, and so on. Write them down on this sheet, and when you have a list of five or more topics, your group leader will write them on the top of separate pieces of newsprint.

Your group leader can help you place the newsprint around the room; then walk around and sign up for interest groups by writing your name on *one* or *two* of the lists. When everyone has signed a list, have a discussion about these common interests.

Section 3

LEARNING ABOUT INVITATIONS

GROUP LEADER INSTRUCTIONS

Summary:

Section 3 introduces the idea of *invitations* as positive messages students can send to themselves and others to form friendships, and contrasts these beneficial messages with *disinvitations,* which often damage relationships that people have. Students will learn the power of their positive and negative behaviors through the phrase "everything counts." No behavior is neutral; everything we do makes either a positive or negative difference to someone.

In addition, this section explores more thoroughly the ideas of *intentional* and *unintentional* behaviors. This lesson will help students learn how their own intentions—the purpose and direction of their behaviors—contribute to the invitations and disinvitations they send to themselves and others.

Objectives

1. To learn about *invitations* and *disinvitations* as positive and negative messages.
2. To learn the differences between intentional and unintentional behaviors.

Activities

Activity 3.1 encourages students to begin a friendship scrapbook. This can be assigned as a homework activity and students can bring in their books periodically throughout the school year to share with one another. The rationale is to have students keep a journal, a record, of friendships they have formed, and to recognize the importance of cherished keepsakes throughout the life span.

Materials

- ❒ Copy of Activity 3.1 for each student
- ❒ *Materials* to help student make a scrap book (paper, string, cardboard, glue). **Note:** In instances where students are instructed to buy scrapbooks, fund-raising strategies may be necessary to help those who cannot purchase their own.

Activity 3.2 encourages students to create positive messages for themselves. The rationale is to emphasize the importance of treating oneself in a positive manner, so that other people will see that you "like yourself."

Materials

- ❒ Copies of Activity 3.2
- ❒ Pencils or pens

Activity 3.3 asks students to think of an invitation they could send to another person, and then to write down reasons why they would *not* send this message. The rationale is to help students explore feelings and thoughts that prevent them from sending positive messages to people with whom they want to be friends.

Materials

- ❒ Copies of Activity 3.3
- ❒ Pencils or pens
- ❒ Chart paper or chalkboard for large group sharing

Activity 3.4 asks students to disclose feelings they have had when someone said or did something disinviting toward them. The rationale is to help students broaden their understanding of how negative messages affect people by examining their own feelings and sharing them with a classmate.

MATERIALS

- ❒ Copy of Activity 3.4
- ❒ Pencils or pens

Activity 3.5 invites students to interview people they know by asking the question, "What is luck?" The rationale is to have students learn many different perceptions of luck and to discover if there is a common link among these divergent perceptions. After students complete their interviews, have the class share the different definitions of "luck" that they compiled. Class discussion can examine commonalities among these definitions and include ways that intention and unintention play a role in these definitions.

MATERIALS

- ❒ Copies of Activity 3.5
- ❒ Pens or pencils
- ❒ Chart paper or chalkboard for large group sharing

Activity 3.6 tells a story about Bobby's first day at school and asks students to determine which characters in the story behaved intentionally or unintentionally. The rationale is to show students that it is difficult for observers to determine whether another person's behaviors are intentional. *Usually, it is only the person himself or herself who knows the intention of a particular behavior.*

MATERIALS

- ❒ Copies of Activity 3.6
- ❒ Pens or pencils

ROLE PLAY

The role-play activity emphasizes the power of words, and why it is important to choose our words intentionally—particularly in difficult situations.

Role Play 3-A. This role play asks students to examine particular words and language used between friends in an argument. The class is asked to write a new script that conveys the same message, but with less harmful language. Ask the class to identify key words that destroy the friendship.

Vocabulary Words

These words may need additional explanation by the group leader depending on the reading level of students in the class. Words with an asterisk denote concepts that may need explanation.

intelligence	miserable
combination	beneficial
insignificant	visible/invisible
criteria*	validated*
automatic	detect

LEARNING ABOUT INVITATIONS

The first step in the art of friendship is to be a friend;
then making friends takes care of itself.

Wilfred A. Peterson

Ever wonder why some people have many friends while others have only a few? There are probably several answers that come to mind. For example, you might think that some people are smarter, better looking, richer, luckier, or more talented than others, and that this helps them have friends. True, some people are smarter, prettier, more talented, or richer, but intelligence, fame, beauty, talent, and wealth do not always equal successful friendships. Sometimes people who are wealthy, pretty, or smart do not have many friends and are not very happy with their lives.

You can probably think of people who have talent, money, fame, or beauty but are not happy or successful in their lives. Perhaps you know someone like this, or maybe you have seen a television character that expresses these feelings—someone about whom people say, "That person has so much talent (or money) and yet is so miserable and unhappy." Sometimes people seem to be on top of the world, but in truth they are unhappy with their lives.

If intelligence, beauty, fame, wealth, or talent do not always add up to success and happiness, what are the conditions that contribute to a successful and happy life? Why are some people successful and happy in their friendships while others are not?

Answers to these questions have been sought for a long, long time, but no simple answers have been found. At best, there is a combination of factors that contribute to success and happiness. Specifically, success and happiness appear to be dependent on how well people communicate and relate with others.

Communicating Successfully

In Dr. William Purkey's book, *Inviting School Success,* he talked about how people—particularly students and teachers—can learn to communicate successfully with one another. He said that people are always sending messages to themselves and others. These messages are sent when people talk and behave in certain ways toward themselves and others. Some messages that people send to themselves and others are helpful and beneficial, while others are harmful and destructive. Dr. Purkey called helpful messages, invitations, and he called harmful messages, disinvitations.

According to this view, successful people send mostly invitations to themselves and others; this is what makes them successful in their friendships. In other words, they "invite" successful relationships. By contrast, people who are unsuccessful in their friendships send and receive too many disinvitations.

So far, you have learned that friendships are chosen, formed, and maintained by the positive actions that you and others take. Now you will learn that these positive actions can take the form of *invitations*. What are these invitations? How are invitations sent? This section will answer these and other questions. To begin, use Activity 3.1 to start a scrapbook.

The kinds of messages people send to themselves and others influence the kinds of friendships they form throughout their lives. How people talk to and behave around others helps to determine how successful their friendships will be. In the remaining sections of this program, you will learn how consistently positive messages can help to develop long-lasting friendships.

An Introduction to Invitations

By studying the messages that people send and receive, researchers have discovered that some messages are very good and helpful while others are not so good, and some are even harmful. Every day, people send and receive hundreds of messages and signals that say to themselves or others that they are important, valuable, and worthwhile people. For example, telling your mom, dad, brother, or sister that you love them sends the message that they are important, valuable, and worthwhile. By preparing for a school test, you send yourself a message that you, too, are important, valuable, and worthwhile. Helping friends to fix a bike, build a dog house, or bake cookies sends similar messages that tell others you care about them and want to be with them.

By the same token, it is sad but true that some people send messages and signals to themselves and others that tell them that they are unimportant, not valuable, and worthless. For example, calling yourself "stupid" because you made a mistake belittles you. In the same way, telling lies about a friend, or teasing your little brother or sister are signals that say they are unimportant and less valuable than you are.

Name ______________________________ Date ______________

ACTIVITY 3.1
Friendship Scrapbook

Take pictures of all your friends and put them in a scrapbook. Write some interesting facts about each of your friends next to their pictures. As you get older, you will have this book, with fond memories of friendships that have touched you in many ways. You can make notes on this activity sheet to plan your scrapbook.

These kinds of messages are called *disinvitations*. Both invitations and disinvitations influence the friendships we have, and we will now explore these messages in greater detail.

Invitations

When people say or do good things for themselves and others, they are sending messages that help them see themselves and others as valuable, capable, and responsible. For example, when your parents say that you've done a good job with a chore around the house, or a friend shares a fruit snack with you, they are sending you *invitations*. When you tell yourself to stay healthy, eat less sugar, study your school assignments, practice your piano playing or your baseball batting, you are inviting yourself to become a better person, student, musician, or baseball player. You can use Activity 3.2 to consider an invitation to yourself.

Invitations are the countless messages, signals, and actions people use to tell themselves and others positive things. Sometimes an invitation may be small and seemingly insignificant, such as helping your dad wash the dishes—or it may be a major event, such as spending time to help your younger brother or sister learn to ride a two-wheel bike for the first time. There are many different kinds and levels of invitations, but all are important and all contribute to the friendships you form in your life.

For example, when you smile at a new neighbor who passes you on the sidewalk, it may seem like an unimportant message, a "tiny" invitation; yet, if no one else has ever smiled at this person before, your smile might be the most important message he or she has ever received! Most people will welcome a sincere smile.

Some invitations are very big and require a great deal of planning, such as saving your allowance several months for a new bike, or working toward an "A" in math! Invitations come in many shapes and sizes, but no matter how big or small they are, all invitations are important. Sometimes people forget that everything they say or do has value, either positive or negative. The lesson to remember about invitations is that *everything counts*. Everything you do or say can make a difference in your life and the lives of others.

Sometimes invitations are obvious, such as a party invitation you receive in the mail. These invitations are visible to you and to others. You can observe them happening and you know who sent them. At other times, invitations are more or less invisible. When you receive an invisible invitation, you do not know who sent it. An example of an invisible invitation would be when you do something helpful around the house, like taking out the garbage—not because your parents asked you to, but simply because you saw that it needed to be done. Later, your mother or father might say, "Who took out the garbage? Thank you. That was very helpful!" Both visible and invisible invitations can be useful in choosing, forming, and keeping friendships.

The more invitations a person receives, the more likely that he or she will feel worthwhile. As a result, people who are frequently invited themselves often send invitations to others. People who feel good about themselves and are confident that

Name ______________________________ Date ______________

ACTIVITY 3.2
Self Invitation

Think of something good you have been meaning to do for yourself. Write down what it is that you have wanted to do. After you have finished writing, share your invitation with a friend and ask your friend to determine if your message is truly a "self" invitation. Your friend should judge the message by these criteria:

- The message is truly beneficial to you.
- The message does not harm anyone else.

Write your message here: ______________________________

You're Invited
Cartoon 3-A

Name ______________________________ Date _______________

ACTIVITY 3.3
Inviting Others

Think of an invitation you could send to another person with whom you want to be friends. Write down this invitation: ______________________________

What, if anything, prevents you from sending this invitation? Write down the reasons why you would not send this message: ______________________________

Sometimes there are no reasons for not sending an invitation except that we are afraid a person might say no. This is a fear of being rejected. With your classmates, discuss this fear and decide whether you think it is a good reason not to send an invitation.

Gold Nugget

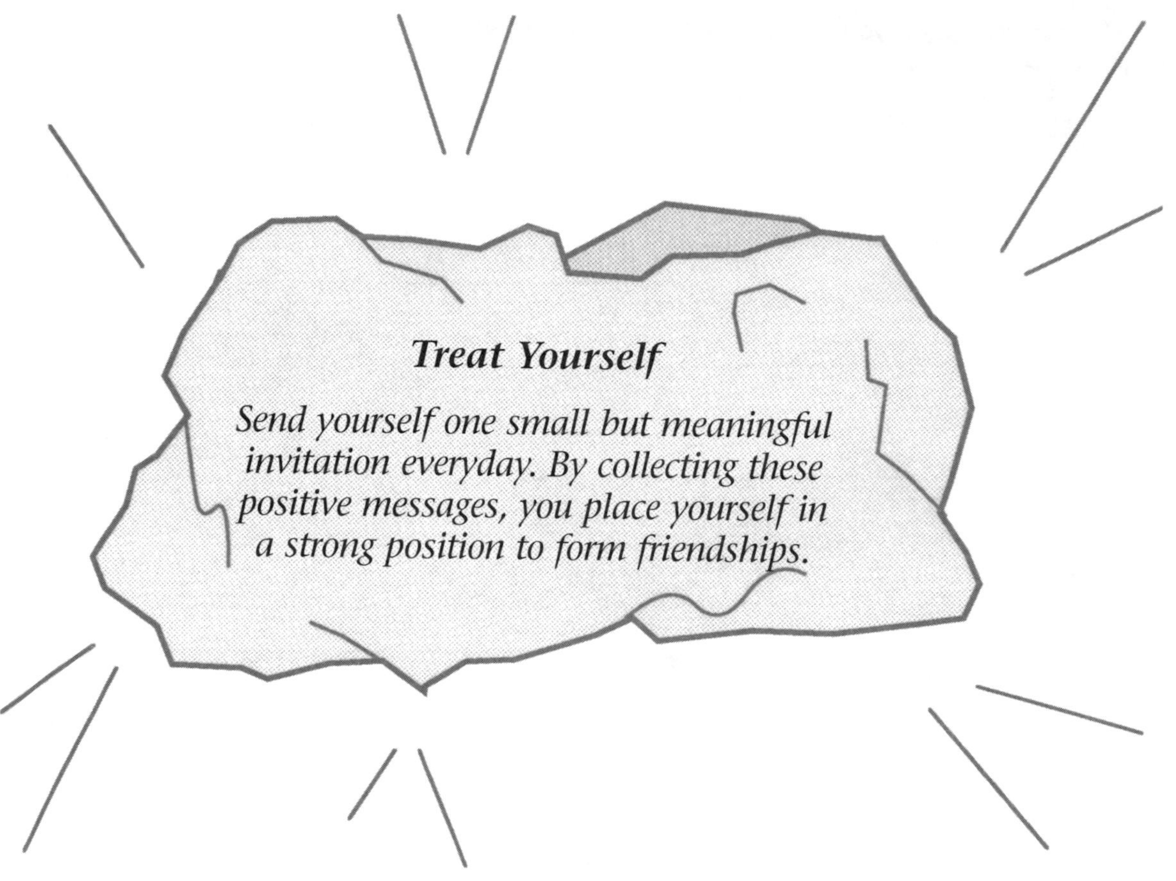

they can be successful usually treat others respectfully, and send many inviting messages to themselves and others. Activity 3.3 will help you send an invitation.

Invitations are sent verbally and nonverbally. Often, people send the most important messages not by what they say to their friends but by how they behave toward them. The saying, "Actions speak louder than words," is true in friendships. More important, the positive things you say must be validated by your behaviors. It is damaging to friendships when people say one thing but do another. For friendships to last, what you say must be consistent with what you do. This is what is meant by being *reliable* and *dependable.* True friends say what they mean, and mean what they say.

Disinvitations

Unfortunately, not all the messages people send and receive are good ones. Sometimes messages and signals can be *disinviting*. These messages tell people that they are no good, dumb, or worthless. Being told that you cannot play on the team because "you do not play well enough," or hitting and hurting someone because you "did not like the way they looked at you" are two examples of harmful and destructive messages.

Just as *everything counts* with invitations, so it is with disinvitations. No disinviting action goes unnoticed or is totally unimportant. The more negative messages people receive, the more likely they are to send negative messages in return. For example, if people keep telling you by their words or actions that you are dumb, eventually you might begin to believe that it is true. You might start telling yourself that you are stupid and cannot do anything right. Eventually, you might stop trying to learn, and that would be very sad. Write your thoughts about a disinvitation in Activity 3.4.

In friendships, you will be successful or unsuccessful based on the invitations or disinvitations you send and receive. It follows that people who disinvite themselves and others most of the time will have difficulty forming and keeping friendships.

There are countless ways that you can invite or disinvite yourself and others. To understand your messages, consider four types of invitations and disinvitations that we call *levels of functioning*:

1. Intentionally Disinviting
2. Unintentionally Disinviting
3. Unintentionally Inviting
4. Intentionally Inviting

Later in Section 4 these four levels of functioning will be referred to as "Four Levels of Encouraging or Discouraging Friendships."

You have already seen examples of invitations and disinvitations, but the words *intentionally* and *unintentionally* are new ones. You learned a little about the importance of intentions in the first section, but here we will examine these two words more closely. To become a truly inviting friend, it is important to know the difference between your intentional behaviors and your unintentional behaviors.

INTENTIONAL BEHAVIORS

The word "intentional" refers to words, behaviors, and actions that are said and done on purpose. You think about them, you know when you say or do them, and you "intend" them to happen. Therefore, when you say or do something intentionally, you mean it!

Invitations Feel So Good
Cartoon 3-B

Name ______________________________ Date ______________

ACTIVITY 3.4
Disinviting Feelings

Think about a time that someone said or did something disinviting toward you. Can you remember the feelings you had? Write down the feelings you remember and share this incident and your feelings with a friend:

The incident: ____

Your feelings: ____

Gold Nugget

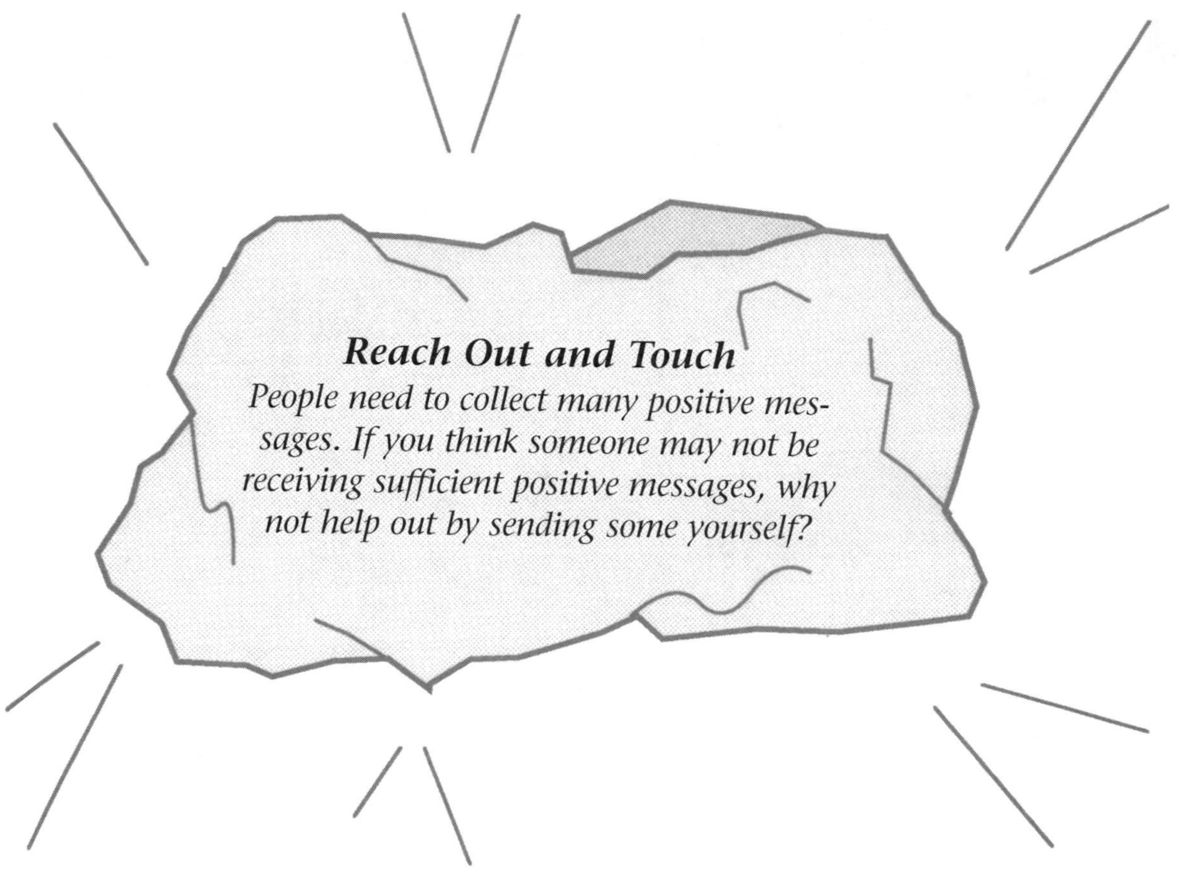

Sometimes your behaviors are intentional because you have taken time to think about them, planned how you were going to act, and then behaved according to your plan. For example, have you ever surprised someone with a present? If so, you will probably remember that you thought about what present you were going to get, where to hide the present so it would not be found, and what "story" you would use to cover up the surprise. When the person expressed surprise, you probably felt satisfied because that's what you *intended.*

On other occasions your behaviors are intentional, not because of your plan, but because past experiences influence your behavior in certain ways. For example, if you know how to ride a bike, you do not think very much about how to ride it. You just get on and do it. You ride your bike *intentionally*, but you do so with such ease and without much thought because past experiences have taught you how to ride without falling off. It seems almost automatic.

Intentional behaviors can also be either positive or negative. As such, they can be either invitations or disinvitations. What they have in common is that they are done with purpose. If you did not mean for them to happen, they would not be intentional. Instead, they would be *unintentional* behaviors.

Unintentional Behaviors

When people say or do something that they do not mean or do not want to happen, they are behaving unintentionally. Have you ever said, "Oh, I didn't mean it!" Sometimes you do not give much thought to your behaviors or you do not plan sufficiently, and as a result, things do not work out as you want them to. If you were planning a picnic of peanut butter and jelly sandwiches and you packed everything but the bread, you might not be too happy with yourself when you opened the basket at the park. You would have made an unintentional mistake, but it would still be frustrating.

Sometimes unintentional behaviors might work out even though not much thought or planning occurred. Have you ever been surprised by how well something turned out and said, "Wow, am I lucky!" You realized that it was not your planning that made the difference, but only your good fortune. Use Activity 3.5 to get other people's ideas about luck.

Intentional and unintentional behaviors exist all around us, and it is not always easy to tell them apart. Even when you think of your own behaviors, it is not always clear whether you mean them! Activity 3.6 tells a story about a new boy at school. See if you can detect which behaviors are intentionally or unintentionally inviting or disinviting.

Darn!
Cartoon 3-C

Name ______________________________ Date ________________

ACTIVITY 3.5
Lucky Interview

Interview people in your school or neighborhood and ask them, "What is luck?" Ask them to give you one sentence about luck. See how many descriptions of luck you compile, and share them in class. Is there any single factor that links all these different descriptions of luck? Use this activity sheet to take notes.

Name ______________________________ Date ______________

ACTIVITY 3.6
Bobby's First Day

Nishiko *[Pronounced NEE-SHEE-KO]* is a ninth-grader from Japan who has been at Dewey High School for three months. One day her algebra teacher, Ms. Parkson, introduces a new boy to the class. She says, "Boys and girls, this is Bobby Richards. He is from another state and is new to our school. Bobby, you may sit at that desk over there."

Nishiko remembers her first day at Dewey and how Ms. Parkson had introduced her with almost exactly the same words, except that she was from another country! She remembers how scared she was walking down the aisle with all the eyes looking at her and realizing that everyone knew her name, but she did not know anyone. She thought, "Will they like me? What do they think about me?" She was so scared!

As Bobby comes down the aisle, Nishiko looks at his eyes. He looks scared too. Bobby sees her eyes and Nishiko smiles at him and says, "Hi. I'm Nishiko. Welcome to our school!" Bobby's face breaks into a wide grin, and he says, "Thanks. "

Whose behaviors were intentional or unintentional, inviting, or disinviting? Write your answers next to the name of each character, and indicate whether or not the behavior was intentional.

Nishiko: ____

____

____

____

____

Bobby: ____

____

____

____

____

Ms. Parkson: ____

____

____

____

____

Discuss your answers with students in your class.

Role Play 3-A
Word Power

Instructions: Your group leader will choose two students to take the roles of friend 1 and friend 2. After they read their scripts quietly to become familiar with their roles, they will role-play the scene. After they are finished, the class can rewrite the script and choose words that are more helpful to the friendship.

Friend 1: Where have you been? You said we would meet right after lunch.

Friend 2: I was talking to Jenny. You won't believe it, she has new roller blades. That's cool.

Friend 1: No, that's stupid. Why would you want to spend time with her? She thinks she's so great. If you like her, then you must be stupid too.

Friend 2: I'm not stupid—you are. What's your problem anyway? Just because I talk to someone else, you get all bent out of shape. Sometimes you act like a jerk.

Friend 1: You're the jerk for letting me wait here for you. I don't need to be with you—so there! *(Walks away.)*

In the story, it is most likely that Nishiko's words were intentionally spoken to help Bobby feel welcomed. She wanted to help him. As you will see later in this program, "wanting to" is an important step in being intentionally inviting.

What did you think about Ms. Parkson's words and behaviors? Were they inviting or disinviting, intentional or unintentional? Actually, we can only guess. Bobby could tell us how he felt when she introduced him, and that might give us a hint as to whether or not he felt invited. Ms. Parkson is the only one who could tell us what her intentions were.

The person *sending* the message controls whether it is intentional or unintentional, but it is the person *receiving* the message who decides whether it is truly inviting or disinviting. This will become clearer in Section 4 when you learn more about the levels of inviting and how people see messages differently. It is these different ways of viewing the messages we receive that help us determine whether they are invitations.

Section 4

FOUR LEVELS OF ENCOURAGING OR DISCOURAGING FRIENDSHIP

GROUP LEADER INSTRUCTIONS

Summary:

Section 4 describes four major levels of inviting (encouraging) and disinviting (discouraging) behaviors. This description combines the ideas of "invitations" and "disinvitations" with the notions of intentional and unintentional behaviors.

This section also explores a new concept of human "perception" and explains how people's perceptions tend to influence how they behave.

Objectives

1. To learn the four levels of inviting and disinviting, and to understand how each person decides at which level he or she will behave.
2. To explore the idea of human perception and the way each person's perceptions influence how he or she behaves.

Activities

Activity 4.1 tells a story of José and Eric and how unintentional actions can affect relationships. This activity demonstrates the power of unintentional behaviors and encourages students to explore alternative actions.

Materials

- ❐ Copies of Activity 4.1
- ❐ Chart paper or chalkboard to record class reactions

Activity 4.2 asks students to think of someone they admire and write a list of characteristics that describe this person. By asking students to compile lists of characteristics they admire in others, they learn about traits and values important to them.

Materials

- ❐ Copies of Activity 4.2
- ❐ Pencils or pens
- ❐ Chart paper or chalkboard for large group sharing

Activity 4.3 asks students to write down a list of reasons why they are friends with a friend. Then students are encouraged to share their lists with the friend (who has also completed a list). This activity helps students compare similarities and differences of perceptions with their friends.

Materials

- ❐ Copies of Activity 4.3
- ❐ Pencils or pens

Activity 4.4 asks students to interview adult friends or relatives and ask them about their friends. The rationale is to have students gather information about why people choose certain friends and learn about common traits such as trust, respect, and so on.

Materials

- ❐ Copies of Activity 4.4
- ❐ Pencils or pens

Activity 4.5 explores the different perceptions people have of the same objects. Students will learn that different perceptions of the same object can often exist. In this activity, the two most common perceptions of the first two objects will be a dog and a horse. The third object is sometimes called "The Old Witch and the Young Lady." Ask how many students can see both of these pictures. Other perceptions of these three objects should be invited and accepted. Ask students to let their imaginations go.

MATERIALS

- ❒ Copies of Activity 4.5

Activity 4.6 asks students to write down privately the title of their favorite TV show. When students are ready, ask them to share and record their responses on a chalkboard. Lead a class discussion about the different shows. This activity reinforces perceptual differences of what is a "favorite" show.

MATERIALS

- ❒ Copies of Activity 4.6
- ❒ Pencils or pens
- ❒ Chalkboard

Activity 4.7 challenges groups of students to answer five questions. Each group must agree on the answer before writing it down and moving on to the next question. When time is up (8 minutes) ask groups to share their answers and record them on a chalkboard. This activity shows how powerful perceptions can sometimes cause us to overlook the facts of a given situation.

MATERIALS

- ❒ Copies of Activity 4.7 for each group
- ❒ Pencils or pens
- ❒ Chalkboard
- ❒ Answers to the questions
  1. If you had only one match and you entered a room in which there were a kerosene lantern, a fireplace, and a wood-burning stove, what would you light first? Answer: *the match*
  2. Do the people living in England have a fourth of July? Answer: Yes, *but they do not celebrate it as Independence Day.*
  3. How many animals of each species did Moses take aboard the Ark with him? Answer: None. *Moses did not build the ark; Noah did.*
  4. Some months have thirty days and some have thirty-one. How many months have twenty-eight days? Answer: *All the months have twenty-eight days, but most have more.*

5. An electric train heads north at 80 miles an hour. The wind is blowing from the east at 20 miles an hour. In what direction will the smoke from the engine point? Answer: *An electric train does not put out smoke.*

Activity 4.8 can become a class project. Doing secretive things to help people feel better about themselves teaches the power of positive actions. Ask the class to create a list of "phantom invitations" that they can use with friends and other people around the school. This activity reinforces the idea that positive messages can have a powerful effect on people's attitudes and behaviors.

MATERIALS

- ❒ Copies of Activity 4.8
- ❒ A list of created "invitations"

ROLE PLAY

Role Play 4-A. The role-play activity asks the class to assess what has happened. Choose two students for the role play—one a shop keeper and the other a shopper. Have the students read their respective roles before the scene begins. Place objects around the classroom, such as pencils, erasers, books, and so forth, that can be part of the "store." At the end of the skit, ask the class to talk about what they saw.

This role play asks two students to pretend they are in a store. One plays the shopkeeper and another plays a customer. The customer is "browsing." At the end of the skit, ask the class what they saw and what they thought about as they watched the role play. Discuss the various perceptions shared by the students.

VOCABULARY WORDS

These words may need additional explanation by the group leader depending on the reading level of students in the class. Words with an asterisk denote concepts that may need explanation.

chronicle
influence*
hesitate
hallmark
perceptive*
intelligence
explanation
nurtured*
dependability*
perception
enrich
significant

FOUR LEVELS OF ENCOURAGING OR DISCOURAGING FRIENDSHIP

Life is a chronicle of friendship.
Friends create the world anew each day.

Helen Keller

So far, you have learned about the differences between invitations and disinvitations and about intentional and unintentional behaviors. Now it is time to combine these elements and look at the four levels of inviting and disinviting behaviors that were introduced in Section 3.

People do not behave the same way all the time. Sometimes they are kind and helpful and sometimes they are thoughtless and hurtful. There are many reasons for this. How people feel about themselves, how busy they are, how tired they might be, or how important something is to them offer a few explanations of why they behave in various ways at different times.

At this point, you are going to learn about the four levels of inviting. Some of these levels are helpful and some are not. People behave at each of the four levels at different times; depending on how they feel, whom they are with, or other reasons. Sometimes people are inviting, and sometimes they are disinviting; sometimes they do things intentionally, and sometimes they do things by accident. This is true for you as well. How you behave *most of the time* greatly influences the friendships you will form with others.

Intentionally Disinviting

The worst level of behaving is to be *intentionally disinviting* toward yourself or others. When people behave this way, they are mean to others because they want to be. They know what they are doing and they do not care about the harm or hurt that is being done. Think of a story you have read or a television show you have watched that told about characters who were intentionally disinviting. What can you say about these characters? How do they behave toward other people? Why do you think they behave that way? Most of the comments you would make about these characters would probably not be very nice. You might have thought that these characters looked scary or mean, and that they were dishonest with other people.

It is difficult to determine why people are intentionally disinviting. Sometimes people have been treated poorly by others for so long that they have come to believe that they are worthless. Because they believe this so strongly, they begin to behave in ways that mistreat other people in return.

All of us are intentionally disinviting on occasion, but most of us behave this way when we are tired, angry, or "trying to get even" with someone who has hurt us. Of course, none of these is a good reason to behave in disinviting ways. In fact, there are no good reasons to send negative, harmful messages to ourselves or others, but sometimes we do.

Gold Nugget

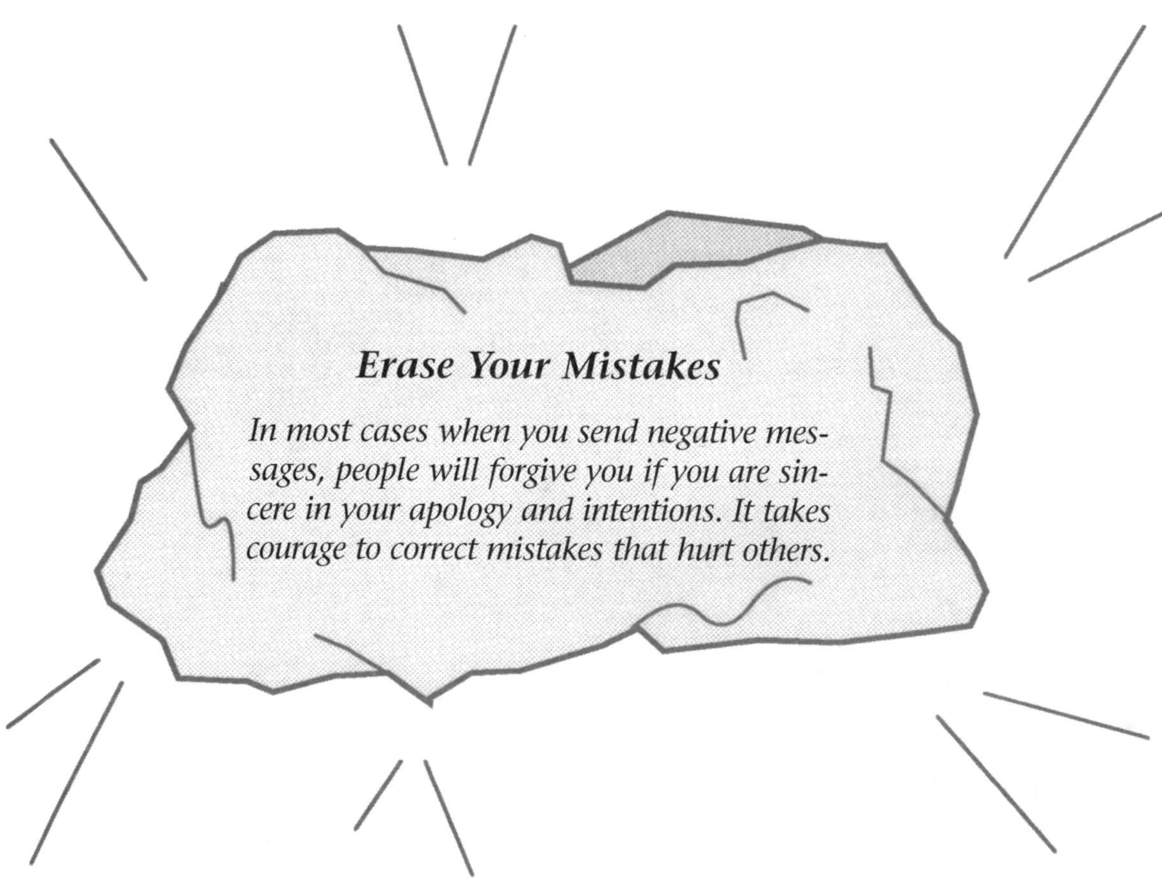

In many situations, disinvitations are easily forgiven, particularly when they involve people about whom you care and who care about you. It takes courage to correct a disinvitation, and *courage* is an important element in becoming a more inviting person. As you saw earlier, it is also important in developing long-lasting friendships.

What about the person who is always intentionally disinviting? Can you do anything to help such a person? It is difficult, but you must try—and keep trying—because everyone in this world is important, and every relationship has the potential to help you. It can be discouraging to try to help someone who is constantly mean and nasty, but on occasion you will make progress, and in some cases, you will help people change their lives. When this happens, it not only helps others, but it is also rewarding to you because you feel so good about it.

You probably have heard or read stories about people who have had difficult lives or have been criminals and they have changed their ways because a "friend" took an interest in them. Sometimes these friends are teachers, counselors, ministers, or other professionals, but at other times it is simply someone who saw a person in need and reached out to help.

People who are intentionally disinviting need someone who cares about them. When they see that another person has taken an interest in their well-being, they begin to behave more kindly toward themselves and others. This change, if nurtured by a good friend, can help any person move to a higher level of behaving.

Unintentionally Disinviting

In many instances, when people disinvite themselves or others, they do not mean it. These types of disinvitations happen by accident, usually because people do not think about their behavior. We call this type of message *unintentionally disinviting*. Read the paragraphs in Activity 4.1, then answer the questions.

All people are unintentionally disinviting at some time or another. When you behave this way, it is likely that you feel bad about it because someone has been hurt due to your carelessness or thoughtlessness. Even though you feel bad, however, you might hesitate to do anything about it. Perhaps you hesitate because you are afraid that the person you have hurt or insulted might be angry, and he or she might not want to make up and be your friend.

Have you ever hurt someone's feelings and been so scared to apologize that you acted as if it never happened? Or did you make up stories to say that you did not do it? Sometimes unintentional disinvitations can quickly become intentional ones if you refuse to accept responsibility for your behaviors. The more stories you tell, the bigger the hole you dig in which to bury your friendships.

Although some disinvitations are unintentional, this does not mean you can overlook them. Unintentional disinvitations can be as harmful as intentional ones. In some instances, they can hurt even more. For example, let's say that a boy in your

Name ______________________________ Date ________________

ACTIVITY 4.1
An Unintentional Disinvitation

José and Eric played baseball on the same team. They both enjoyed baseball, and although they were not close friends, they respected each other's ability. The only time they saw each other was when the team practiced or played a game because José went to public school and Eric attended a private school. Most of the other players on the team went to José's school. One day after practice, José asked several of his teammates if they would come to his house the next day to meet his uncle who was a major league baseball player. His family was having a small party and told José he could invite some friends. Eric overheard José inviting other players to meet his famous uncle, and left the practice disappointed because he was not asked.

Reactions

1. If you were Eric, how would you have felt in this situation? ______________________

____

____

____

2. What would you have done, if you were Eric? ______________________

____

____

____

3. What do you think about José? ______________________

____

____

____

4. If you were José, would you have done anything differently? ______________________

____

____

____

school is cruel to everyone; he is intentionally disinviting. Every time he sees you he does something mean, calls you a name, or makes a face at you. You have come to expect it—to the point that it does not bother you as much as it first did. You have learned to ignore his insulting behaviors.

Now let us say another student, a girl who is your friend, forgets to invite you to a party she is having. How would you feel? If you really cared about going to the party, chances are you would be hurt because you did not receive an invitation. In fact, the hurt would probably be more painful than the insults you received from the boy, because you had come to expect his insults but valued her friendship. When a friend unintentionally disinvites, you might feel totally neglected.

As with the other levels of inviting, unintentional disinvitations happen to all of us at some time or other. All people behave this way on occasion. Even though these negative messages are unintentional, they can do as much harm as intentional ones. For this reason, it is important to avoid behaviors that are unintentionally disinviting to yourself and others.

Unintentionally Inviting

Sometimes messages bring positive results even though they have occurred by accident. When this happens, the sender is being *unintentionally inviting.*

Have you ever had people thank you for helping them, even though you really didn't have them in mind when you did it? For example, in the springtime you want to ride your bicycle, but when you go to get it out of the storage shed, you find a mess of boxes, lawn equipment, and other stuff piled up in front of the bike. Without much thought, you clean away the boxes, put the tools back in their proper places, and take the bike out for a ride. Later that day your dad comes to you and says, "Thank you so much for cleaning up the shed. It was a job I was meaning to do, and you really helped me."

Do you *feel* a little uncomfortable with his praise? Maybe a little. But do you tell him the truth—that you were only trying to get your bike out? Heavens no! Dad feels good. So what if you did not mean it? It worked out great, right? Why spoil a good thing by telling him?

Occasionally people do things that work out very well even though they do not know why. When this happens, they are behaving at a level called *unintentionally inviting.*

You might ask at this point, what is wrong with unintentional invitations? If these are positive messages and they help people, what is wrong with them? Well, nothing is wrong with them because they do help people; however, this program is about inviting friendships, and one thing about forming and keeping friendships that you have already learned is that you have to work at them. Good friendships do not develop by accident. You have to want them, plan for them, and make them happen. Quality friendships are formed intentionally. So you see, if you always are unintentional, then you do not know what you are doing to help your friendships. Without this knowledge, you cannot repeat positive behaviors that help you form lasting friendships.

Unintentional invitations are nice because they have positive outcomes. People feel good and appreciate what you have done for them. To form friendships, however, you must consistently search for ways to be with other people and share their lives. Too many unintentional behaviors do not help you be consistent. When you are inconsistent with your behaviors, people soon learn that they cannot *depend* on you. To discover the behaviors you would like to demonstrate, use Activity 4.2.

Dependability is an important element of being an inviting friend. If people find they can depend on you, it is likely they will want to form strong friendships. As you learned earlier, a good friend is one whom you can trust under any circumstances. Dependability helps you develop this trust among friends. Once you have the courage to correct your mistakes and maintain a level of dependable behavior, you are more likely to function at the highest level—*intentionally inviting.*

Gold Nugget

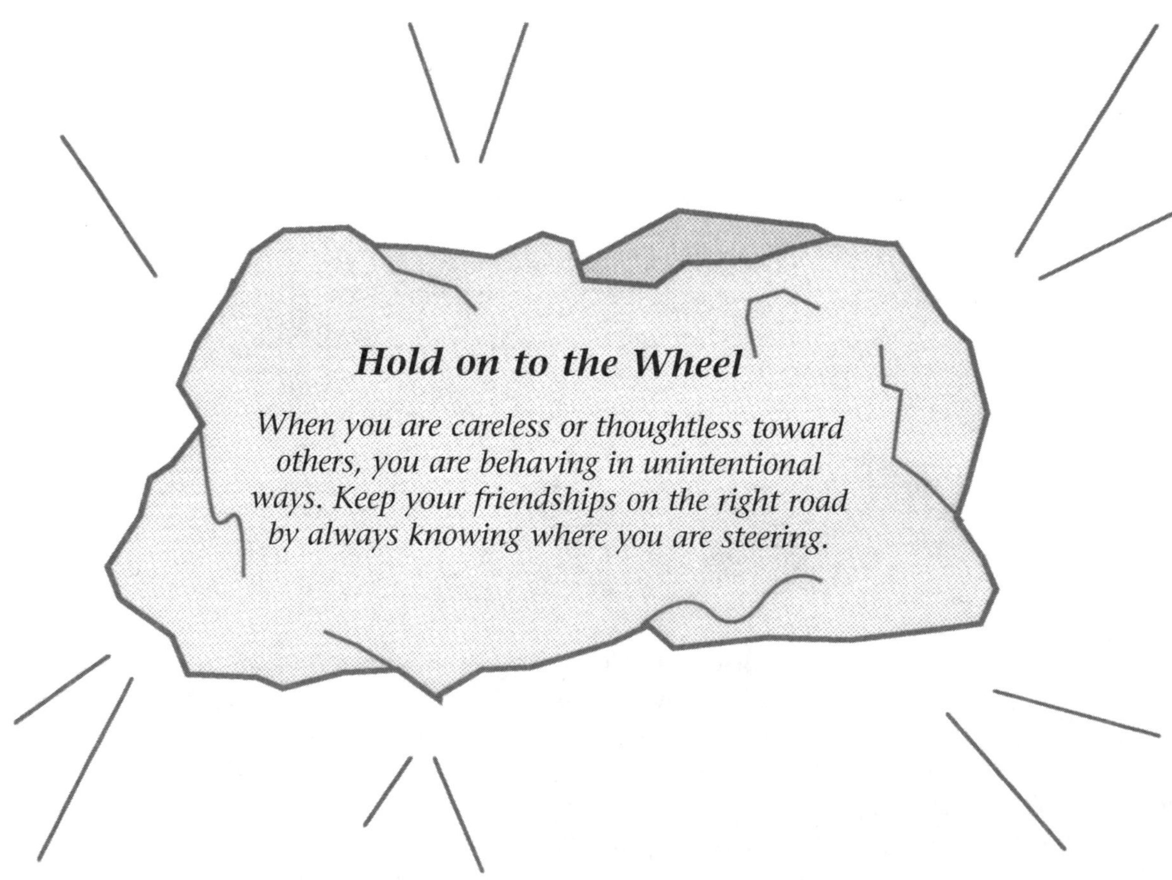

Name ______________________________ Date ______________

ACTIVITY 4.2
Inviting Qualities

Think of someone that you admire—someone who has many friends and of whom other people speak well. Write a list of characteristics that describe this person. Compare your list with a classmate's and see how many of the characteristics are the same. By compiling your lists, you will create a description of a most valued person and friend. You can add characteristics from your classmate's list if you admire them, too.

Characteristics of someone I admire: ______________________________

Intentionally Inviting

Do you know people who "have it all together"? They are pleasant to be around and they have many friends. Do you know any people who are like this? If so, you know that they are people who treat others with thoughtfulness and respect. They are truly intentionally inviting.

So far, you have learned about two characteristics of being an inviting person—courage and dependability. It is time to learn about some of the other qualities that will help you become intentionally inviting in your friendships. Do Activity 4.3 with a friend. As you read about these qualities, compare them with the list you compiled in Activity 4.2.

People who are intentionally inviting behave with a high level of *responsibility*. They take charge of their lives, rarely make excuses for their mistakes, and refuse to blame others for the problems they have. Being a responsible person requires an *optimistic* view of one's life, an ability to earn the *trust* of others and to trust in return, a strong *respect* for oneself and others, and, as you have seen, the ability to be intentional with one's behaviors. People can maintain a high level of intentionally inviting behaviors if they have a positive view of their lives, have faith that changes can be made in those things that need to be changed, have a high regard for their own abilities, value other people, and develop close, trusting relationships.

You may remember at this point that the qualities of *courage, dependability, optimism, trust,* and *respect* were mentioned in Section 1 as important elements in choosing, forming, and keeping friendships. To these qualities we have now added *responsibility* and *intentionality*. When friendships collapse, it is because one or more of these elements has been lost. Maintaining lasting friendships requires intentional behaviors that focus on the important qualities found in invitations. Activity 4.4 will help you focus on these qualities.

Friendships and invitations are also related because of the perceptions of the people involved. Perceptions are defined as the ways that people see, understand, and learn about the things around them. This perceptual learning takes place through all of your senses. How you see, hear, feel, and smell things helps you to *perceive* everything around you. To fully understand invitations and friendships, you want to understand your own perceptions as well as the perceptions of others.

Perceiving and Inviting

Have you ever watched a movie, play, or skit at school, and when it was over you and your friends disagreed about whether it was good or bad? You may have said, "What a great movie!" and your friends may have looked at you in a weird way and said, "What? Are you nuts? That was a stupid movie!" You all saw the same event, at the same time, and in the same place. Why did you not have the same opinion

Name ______________________________ Date ______________

ACTIVITY 4.3
Friendship List

Ask a friend to make a list of all the reasons why he or she is your friend. At the same time, you make your list. When you are both finished, compare your lists and see how many of the items are similar or the same. Compare these lists with those you made in Activity 4.2

My Friend Is:

Name ______________________________ Date ________________

ACTIVITY 4.4
History Lesson

Ask adults to tell you about their friends when they were your age. Talk with grandparents, neighbors, or teachers. Ask them to tell you why they were friends with these persons. Listen as they tell you about their friends and see if they mention the qualities of trust, respect, dependability, optimism, and responsibility. You can use this page to make notes.

Gold Nugget

of it? To understand why this happens, you must first have an understanding of what *perceptions* are and how people form them. Check your perceptions with Activity 4.5.

When you were born, you came into the world without any knowledge or experiences. This is true for everyone. It is as if your life began as an empty balloon. Quickly you started to have experiences, and you used your senses to learn about the world, understand it, and draw conclusions about your experiences in it. You heard the voices of your parents and other people, saw objects, felt people touching you, and smelled fragrances. These experiences began to fill your perceptual world (your balloon), much like the drawing in Figure 4A. Sometimes you might have rejected an experience, and not let that one into your balloon. In this way, you used your perceptual ability to form a world that is uniquely yours.

Name ______________________ Date ______________

ACTIVITY 4.5
What Do You See?

Look at the pictures below and write down what you see. Compare your perceptions with those of other students in your class.

1

2

____

____

____

____

3

____

____

____

[1]Original graphic by John J. Schmidt.

[2]This graphic is an adaptation of the "Horse and Rider" in *Light and Vision* (1969) by Time-Life Books, NY.

[3]Created by W. E. Hill, this picture was originally published in *Puck,* November 6, 1915, and has since been reprinted in numerous works to demonstrate how more than one object can be found in a single picture.

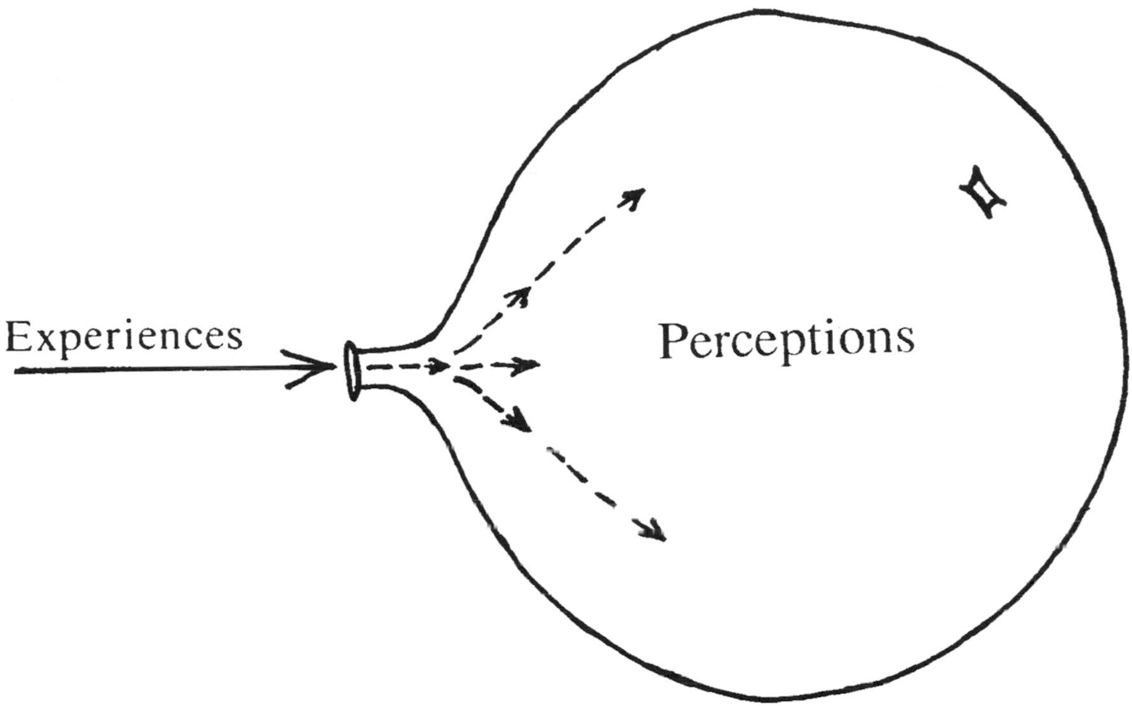

Figure 4-A

On the basis of the number and kinds of experiences accumulated over time, you formed certain perceptions and opinions about yourself and your world, and today these opinions help guide your behaviors. The more experiences you have the more expanded your views are, and the more enriched your life becomes. In a way, this too is similar to a balloon. If you blow up a balloon just a little and let it go, it will not fly very far. But if you keep blowing it up very large and let it go, it will fly much farther. So it is with perceptions and experiences. The more experiences you have, the wider your choices of behaviors can be.

When you release the air in your balloon, it flies differently from anyone else's balloon, just as your perceptions guide you differently than other people's perceptions guide them. That is why people's perceptions of the same or similar events often disagree with the perceptions of their friends, or even of their brothers and sisters.

Role Play 4-A
Perceptions

Instructions: Your leader will choose two students to take the roles of a storekeeper and customer. They will read their scripts quietly and become familiar with their assigned roles, then play the scene. After they are finished, the class can discuss what they saw and what they thought was going on in the scene.

Storekeeper: *(walking around the shop, dusting and straightening items on the shelves)*

Customer: *(walks into the store and begins looking around)*

Storekeeper: Hello. Is there anything I can help you with?

Customer: *(acts a little nervous, looking around to see who is watching)* No, I'm just looking.

Storekeeper: *(goes back to dusting and straightening, and keeps watching the customer)*

Customer: *(keeps walking around picking up items and then putting them down; occasionally, glances over at the storekeeper)*

Storekeeper: *(after a few minutes)* I have some new books in. Are you interested?

Customer: No, I'm just looking. *(walks over to particular item and picks it up; looks around and walks to another area of the store with the item in hand)*

Storekeeper: *(looks over at the customer and says)* Do you want to buy that?

Customer: No thanks. *(puts the item down and walks out of the store)*

Each person's world is unique. No one else sees his or her world exactly as you see yours. As a result, people perceive the same things and events a little differently. These differences can either enrich relationships or invite conflict. They enrich relationships when people are willing to look at other points of view and, if appropriate, change their perspective about certain issues. As people are willing to accept new experiences and new knowledge into their worlds, they are able to form new perceptions. Sometimes you call this "changing your mind." When you change your mind to include perceptions that are similar to those of your friends, it strengthens your friendships.

Perceptions not only help you create messages to send to yourself and others, they also help you interpret the messages that you receive from other people. Learning about your perceptions and the differences you have with people who are close to you is important. It is particularly important in understanding who you are and why you feel and behave the way you do. Knowing yourself is the first step in getting to know others. To form significant friendships you must know about yourself. You can use Activities 4.6 and 4.7 to learn more about your perceptions, as well as those of your classmates.

Who are you? What do you think about yourself? How do you feel about yourself? The answers to these questions form the sum of all the perceptions you have about yourself. This sum is called your *self-concept.* In the next section you will learn about your self-concept and how it develops and guides your behaviors.

To reinforce what you have learned in this section about inviting and disinviting, you can have fun with Activity 4.8.

Name ______________________________ Date ________________

ACTIVITY 4.6
"TV Hodgepodge"

Write down the name of your favorite TV show. Do it privately; don't show it to anyone. When everyone has finished writing, you can all share what you wrote down. Your group leader will keep a list on the chalkboard as you report. When everyone has reported, have a class discussion on the different types of favorite programs listed. You may want to make some notes on this sheet to prepare for the class discussion.

Name ______________________________ Date ______________

ACTIVITY 4.7
Perceptive Intelligence

Your group leader will divide you into several groups with four to five students in each group. Each group must answer the following questions. One member of each group will lead the discussion and write down the group's answer. Your group must come to agreement about each question before writing down your answer. You will have 8 minutes for the activity.

1. If you had only one match and you entered a room in which there were a kerosene lantern, a fireplace, and wood-burning stove, what would you light first? ________________

   ____

   ____

   ____

2. Do the people living in England have a fourth of July? ________________

   ____

   ____

   ____

3. How many animals of each species did Moses take aboard the ark with him? __________

   ____

   ____

   ____

4. Some months have thirty days and some have thirty-one. How many months have twenty-eight days? ______________________________

   ____

   ____

   ____

5. An electric train heads north at 80 miles an hour. The wind is blowing from the east at 20 miles an hour. In what direction will the smoke from the engine point? ____________

   ____

   ____

   ____

After groups have responded and answers have been recorded on a chalkboard, share the correct answers. Discuss how perceptions influenced the groups' answers to the questions.

Name ______________________________ Date ________________

ACTIVITY 4.8
The Phantom Inviter

Do some secretive things for your friends. Mail them funny cards, but send them unsigned. Put pieces of candy on their desks at school for a midday treat. There are numerous positive messages you can plan and, who knows, maybe it will catch on and others will begin sending "phantom invitations." Ask your teacher about sending "phantom invitations" to students in other classes in the school. Write your ideas on this activity sheet.

Section 5

KNOWING YOUR SELF

GROUP LEADER INSTRUCTIONS

Summary:

This section teaches students about *self-concept*—how it is developed and how it changes. Students will learn about different parts of the self, including the physical self, emotional self, and behavioral self. They will also examine *facts* and *beliefs* that influence the development of their self-concepts.

The second half of this section explores how the self-concept relates to friendships and invitations. Students will learn how the friends they choose are reflections of *themselves*. In addition, they will learn how the inviting and disinviting messages they choose to send both to themselves and to others relate to the perceptions they have of themselves and the world around them.

Objectives

1. To learn about the self-concept—how it develops and changes.
2. To understand how perceptions about oneself influence the messages one chooses to send.
3. To learn that some of the most important invitations a person creates and sends are those given to oneself.

Activities

Activity 5.1 asks students to identify different parts of themselves. This activity reinforces the belief that there are a multitude of aspects that make up a person's self-concept.

Materials

- ❒ Copies of Activity 5.1
- ❒ Pens and pencils
- ❒ Chart paper or chalkboard to record class reactions

Activity 5.2 has students evaluate aspects of their physical selves and compare these "facts" with feelings they have about those physical traits. By exploring these feelings and sharing perceptions with other students, they learn that it is often their perceptions, and *not* the physical trait, that influences their feelings and other behaviors. Sharing with other students can also demonstrate that these feelings are common among children their age.

Materials

- ❒ Copies of Activity 5.2
- ❒ Pencils or pens

Activity 5.3 asks students to read a list of behaviors and write down those they use often. Then, for each behavior students should indicate whether a particular behavior is helpful in making friends. The rationale is to have students evaluate some of their behaviors.

Materials

- ❒ Copies of Activity 5.3
- ❒ Pencils or pens

Activity 5.4 invites students to create pictures of their self-concepts. After they have drawn their pictures, ask them to share with a classmate. Discuss similar characteristics as well as unique aspects in the drawings created by students. Sometimes creative exercises can help students become more aware of their perceptions and learn more about themselves.

Materials

- ❒ Copies of Activity 5.4
- ❒ Pens, pencils, crayons, or other art media

Activity 5.5 instructs students to make a list of the seven most important things in their lives. Once the original list is completed, students are asked to compare their list with a classmate's and look for similarities and differences. After that comparison, students are asked to cross off three (3) things on their list and compare again with the classmate. This activity shows students what things are most important to them, and the priority they give to those important things.

MATERIALS

- ❒ Copies of Activity 5.5
- ❒ Pens or pencils

Activity 5.6 invites students to write a résumé about themselves as if they were applying for a friendship. This activity helps students clarify those traits about themselves they believe are their strengths—those that are most helpful in forming friendships

MATERIALS

- ❒ Copies of Activity 5.6
- ❒ Pens or pencils
- ❒ Sample résumés for students to use as models

ROLE PLAYS

Role Play 5-A asks students to act out different feelings in front of a mirror. The class might do this by having students act out feelings in front of the class and have classmates guess what the feelings are. Students are also asked to pretend that they feel one way but act the opposite.

Role Play 5-B asks students to go on a treasure hunt and look for "treasured" traits about their classmates. Students write down one positive and one negative characteristic about themselves, and they write a number from 1 to 5 next to each trait. Next, students put headings for two columns on their papers. One column heading is *Positive*; the other is *Negative*. When every student has written two characteristics with assigned numbers and written the two column headings on a piece of paper, the role-play begins.

Everyone gets up and walks around the room trying to find *positive* characteristics. For example, one student would approach another and say, "Number 2." If the second student has not numbered either characteristic as number 2, the first student says, "Sorry," and moves on to another student. If the second student says, "friendly" or some other positive characteristic, however, that means the number was correct and the characteristic was "friendly." The first student writes down the characteristic on his or her list under the *Positive* heading and moves on.

When a student guesses a correct number, but the second student gives a negative characteristic, the receiving student must write it down in the *Negative* column. As soon as a student has five more positive characteristics than negative characteristics he or she yells, "I found the Treasure!"

Vocabulary Words

These words may need additional explanation by the group leader depending on the reading level of students in the class. Words with an asterisk denote concepts that may need explanation.

virtue*
contrast
emotional
characteristics
sulking
attentive*
disrupting
résumé

vice*
psychological*
illustrate*
hygiene
personalized*
alter
numerous
assessing

KNOWING YOUR SELF

If it is a virtue to love my neighbor as a human being,
it must be a virtue—and not a vice—to love myself,
since I am a human being too.

Erich Fromm

The sum of the beliefs and feelings that people have about themselves is called the *self-concept*. Your self-concept is everything you believe to be true about you. If you believe that you are valued by other people, then that belief, along with countless others, becomes part of your *self*, and guides your behaviors. In contrast, if you think you are *not* valued by other people, that perception is an equally powerful influence in how you choose to behave toward yourself and others.

Have you looked in the mirror lately? Take a few minutes, find a mirror, and look at yourself. Take your time; look yourself over really well.

What did you see? "Myself," did you say? That's right! Actually, what you saw in the mirror was your *physical* self. You saw your body—your face, arms, legs, hands, feet, and other features—all your visible parts that make up the physical "you." There are other parts of yourself that you cannot see by looking in a mirror, and they are just as important to who you are as is your physical self.

In this section, you will learn about the *self*, how it is created, and how it changes. Learning about yourself can help you become more aware of your abilities, behaviors, and feelings. This knowledge helps you understand what other people think about you and why they want, or do not want, to be your friend. To understand what your *self* is, it will help to define what the *self* means.

What Is the Self?

You saw what is meant by the physical self when you looked in the mirror. Can you think of some other parts of yourself? Depending on how specific you want to be, you can create an endless list. See how many parts you can list in Activity 5.1.

Name ______________________________ Date ______________

ACTIVITY 5.1
Self Parts

List all the parts of your *self:*

____

____

____

____

____

____

____

____

____

____

____

____

____

____

____

Compare the list you made with the list below.

physical self (body)

emotional self (feelings)

social self (friendships)

behavioral self (actions)

athletic self (sports)

educated self (studies)

committed self (values and beliefs)

vocational self (jobs and careers)

psychological self (intelligence and mental health)

As you can see from the list in Activity 5.1, there are many parts of the self and each part is important in its own way. The parts are all related to one another. For example, your *behavioral self* (how you behave) is related to your *emotional self* (how you feel). You can probably think of times when your behavior was silly because you felt like having fun. At other times, you may have behaved angrily because you were angry with someone. Each part of your *self* is related in some way to one or more of the other parts.

In this section, we will focus on three major parts of the self: the physical self, the emotional self, and the behavioral self. Before learning about these three parts, you should know one more thing about the self. The self consists of *facts* about you as well as *beliefs* you hold to be true about yourself.

Facts and Beliefs

Your *self* is made up of important parts, and each part consists of two elements: facts and beliefs. Facts are the things you know about yourself. Beliefs, on the other hand, are the ideas you hold to be true about those facts. For example, what are some facts of your physical self? Are you a boy or girl? What is your skin color? What is the color of your eyes? Your hair? The answers to these questions provide some facts about your physical self. These facts are real and usually cannot be changed. If you are a boy, you will grow up to be a man. If you are a girl, you will become a woman. You cannot change the color of your eyes (although some people wear tinted contact lenses), and if you are challenged by a physical loss, such as the loss of an arm or leg, you will always have that physical difference.

Beliefs are the thoughts you have about facts. While facts, such as those related to the physical self, make up a large part of yourself, it is the beliefs you have about those facts that give direction to your life. By returning to the examples of the physical self, we can illustrate this point.

Are you a boy or girl? Whichever you are, it is a fact. Now, what do you think about being a boy or a girl? Do you believe it is better to be a boy or a girl? Your answers to these questions help to determine the beliefs you have that make up an important part of your *self*. As you learn about your physical, emotional, and behavioral self, be mindful about the differences between your facts and your beliefs about each of these characteristics.

Physical Self. The physical self, as you learned above, consists of all your bodily parts and, in addition, the beliefs that you have about your physical appearance. Questions about how tall you are, the color of your hair, what you weigh, how many fingers you have, and how big your nose is are all related to the physical self. At the same time, your beliefs about the answers to these questions make up a value system that is also related to your physical self.

We all have beliefs about our physical selves. Most people would like to be taller or shorter, heavier or skinnier, handsomer or prettier. Sometimes these beliefs are very strong. On occasion, they are so strong that they prevent people from forming friendships. For example, sometimes people think that they are not the right size and therefore no one would want to be their friend. Because they believe this so strongly, they avoid other people. They do not speak to them; they do not even look at other people because they are afraid others will not like them. If you act this way, people think that you do not like them. As a result, they stay away from you. They do not talk to you and do not invite you to be their friend.

People who are comfortable with their physical selves do not worry about what others think about how they look. As a result, they are more willing to take the risk of approaching others to be their friends. It may be true that some people will make fun of the way you look, but only when you *believe* their insults will your physical self affect your friendships. Use Activity 5.2 to explore your feelings about your physical self.

Acceptance of your physical self is a first step toward having others accept you. It is also a first step in making friends. When people find that you are comfortable

Gold Nugget

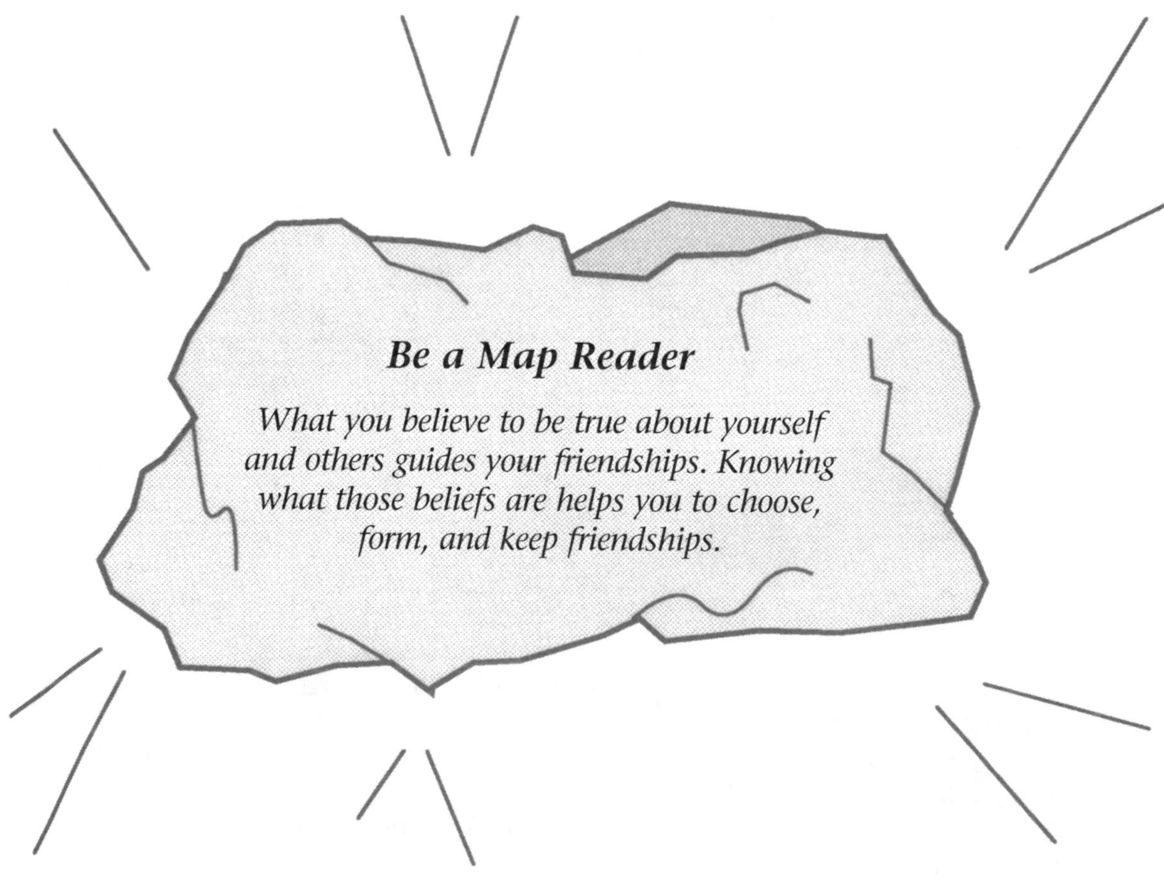

Name ______________________________ Date ________________

ACTIVITY 5.2
Assessing Your Physical Self

Write down physical traits about yourself in the *Fact* column and next to each trait, write down your beliefs about them in the *Feeling* column.

Fact	Feeling
______________________________	______________________________
______________________________	______________________________
______________________________	______________________________
______________________________	______________________________
______________________________	______________________________
______________________________	______________________________
______________________________	______________________________
______________________________	______________________________
______________________________	______________________________
______________________________	______________________________
______________________________	______________________________
______________________________	______________________________
______________________________	______________________________
______________________________	______________________________
______________________________	______________________________
______________________________	______________________________
______________________________	______________________________
______________________________	______________________________
______________________________	______________________________
______________________________	______________________________

One aspect about our beliefs is that they are highly influenced by our perceptions. Check your feelings out with a close friend by sharing your lists. See if your friend has similar feelings about his or her physical traits. You can use the rest of the page to write about sharing with your friend.

Remember: You may not be able to change your physical traits, but only *you* control your feelings about them.

with your appearance—you accept the way you look—most of them will look beyond your physical self to get to know the whole person you are. The few people who cannot get beyond your physical appearance probably would not make the best of friends for you regardless of how good you looked.

Of course, you do want to take care of yourself by practicing good hygiene and grooming. These are ways of inviting yourself as well as others personally. You will learn more about inviting yourself personally later in this guide.

True friends care about you because of what they find in other parts of your *self*. In particular, true friends care about how you feel and behave toward them. Your feelings and behaviors toward others are influenced by beliefs and facts related to your *emotional self* and your *behavioral self*.

Emotional Self. The emotional self is the part of your self-concept that guides your feelings. Your expressed and unexpressed feelings are all part of your emotions. The emotional self allows you to express sadness, happiness, anger, joy, and many other feelings. It also helps you decide whether or not to express any feelings openly, depending on the situation you are in.

As with the physical self, your emotional self can be viewed in two parts: facts and beliefs. The facts are the emotions you express outwardly as well as inwardly. Sometimes the emotions people express on the outside are not the same as the emotions they are feeling on the inside. Have you ever felt sad, but not wanting others to know it, pretended to be happy? The fact was that people saw you as happy, but you knew you were sad. Both emotions existed because you wanted them to.

Often people disguise their true feelings because of the beliefs they have about particular emotions. What you believe about your emotions is as important as the emotions themselves. Your beliefs, as we have seen with the physical self, guide the emotional self and help you to decide which feelings to express. A story about a young boy shows how this is so.

BIG BOYS DON'T CRY

The boy went to a very popular movie with a group of adults. The movie was both joyful and sad. After the movie ended, the people were walking out of the theater and the boy said to one of the men, "Why were you crying?" The man replied, "It was a joyous movie and I was moved to tears." The boy thought for a moment and said, "Well, I didn't cry." The man looked at him and said, "That's okay. People show their emotions in different ways, and it is all right that you didn't cry." They continued walking, and the boy spoke up again, "Well, I had one tear, but I held it back!" What the boy seemed to be saying was that he felt the same emotion, but because he believed that "men shouldn't cry," he held back any expression of the emotion he felt.

The story shows how powerful our beliefs can be in influencing behaviors. Frequently, people behave in certain ways, not because of what is fact, but because of what they believe to be true. This point is emphasized in the description of the behavioral self.

Behavioral Self. People have many behaviors that make up their behavioral selves. Think of the different behaviors you have used today. Need a list? Try the list that follows and see how many of these behaviors you used today:

reading	arguing	eating
sleeping	loving	working
pretending	helping	daydreaming
fighting	smiling	laughing
studying	avoiding	hating
talking	lying	praying
running	playing	relaxing
sulking	stealing	worrying
gossiping	hugging	observing

The list could go on and on. How many did you use today? The behaviors that you checked are facts. You actually used them. You know you did. They are facts, and as you have learned about other parts of the self, these facts are important to your behavioral self. So are your beliefs. As noted earlier, the beliefs you have about a particular emotion or behavior influence whether you accept or deny what you feel. For example, have you ever been afraid of something, but you worried more about what other people would think if you admitted your fear? You can use Activity 5.3 to explore your behaviors and your beliefs about them.

Role Play 5-A
Give a Performance

Instructions: Students will volunteer to look in a mirror and act out different feelings. The group leader will say, "See yourself. This is the way that others see you." Next, your leader will ask some students to pretend that inside they feel unhappy, but on the outside they are trying not to show it, and then ask the class, "How do they look?" Different students can try doing this with other feelings like anger, disappointment, excitement, and others. They can practice in front of a mirror first and then perform in front of the class. The rest of the class will guess what the "real" feeling is.

Name ______________________ Date ____________

ACTIVITY 5.3
Beliefs About My Behaviors

Look at the list of behaviors on p. 99, and in the *Behavior* column write down the ones you use often. Then in the *Belief* column indicate whether or not this behavior helps you make friends.

Behavior	Belief

I'm NOT Scared
Cartoon 5-A

Behaviors that you believe are important are the ones that you will use most often. For example, if you think smiling is good for relationships, then you will smile. On the other hand, if you think frowning will help you get your way, then you will frown often. The beliefs you have about your behaviors play an important role in the friendships you form. They also play an important role in determining how lasting your friendships will be. This can be seen in the story of Naomi *(Pronounced NYE-O-MEE).*

NAOMI THE FIBBER

Naomi was a very likable girl who made many friends in school and in her neighborhood. She often approached new children and welcomed them to school or her neighborhood. Naomi acted very friendly toward them and this behavior won her many new friends. Unfortunately, her friendships did not last a very long time. In part, this was due to Naomi's strong belief that she was going to lose all her friends. In order not to lose them, Naomi would use fibbing behaviors to exaggerate her own importance.

One day her friend Joshua said that his dad was buying a new car. Naomi replied that her dad also was buying a new car and it was going to be "very expensive." Later, Joshua found out that Naomi's dad was not buying a car at all. He began to doubt Naomi's sincerity and when she sensed this, she began telling more fibs to win back his friendship. You can guess what happened. Naomi's fibs turned Joshua away from her, and their friendship ended.

The behaviors you choose and the beliefs you have play a vital role in the friendships you make and keep. All of the various parts of yourself—all the facts and beliefs—combine to form a view that is called your *self-concept.* Your self-concept and all its parts help to determine the kinds of friendships you will form.

Now that you understand what the self-concept is and how it influences your friendships, you will learn how people develop self-concepts. The self-concept is not something that you can see or touch; it is simply an idea of how people use their perceptions to develop a view of themselves and others.

WHERE DOES THE SELF COME FROM?

The self-concept is learned. From the time you were born until the time you die, you learn things about yourself, the world, and the people around you. This learning is made up of all your experiences and the meaning that you give to those experiences. Earlier in this program you learned that your perceptions are the ways you see and understand things around you. Your perceptions help you give meaning to your experiences.

People perceive their experiences through all of their senses. Everything you see, hear, touch, smell, and taste is evaluated and brought into your world of experiences. This world of experiences, with its own personalized meaning, is your self-concept. Because your perceptions differ from those of other people, your senses provide different evaluations of similar experiences. You can see this by noting how people prefer a wide variety of music, like different fragrances, and enjoy the tastes of many types of foods. Because of these differences, self-concepts are unique. No two people have self-concepts that are exactly alike.

Because your self-concept consists of things you have learned from all of your life's experiences, it takes a while for it to be fully developed. This does not mean that your early experiences in life are unimportant. On the contrary, many of the opinions you have formed about yourself early in life will continue unchanged for many years, and maybe for as long as you live. For this reason, your early years of growing up are very important to becoming a healthy person. They are particularly important

Gold Nugget

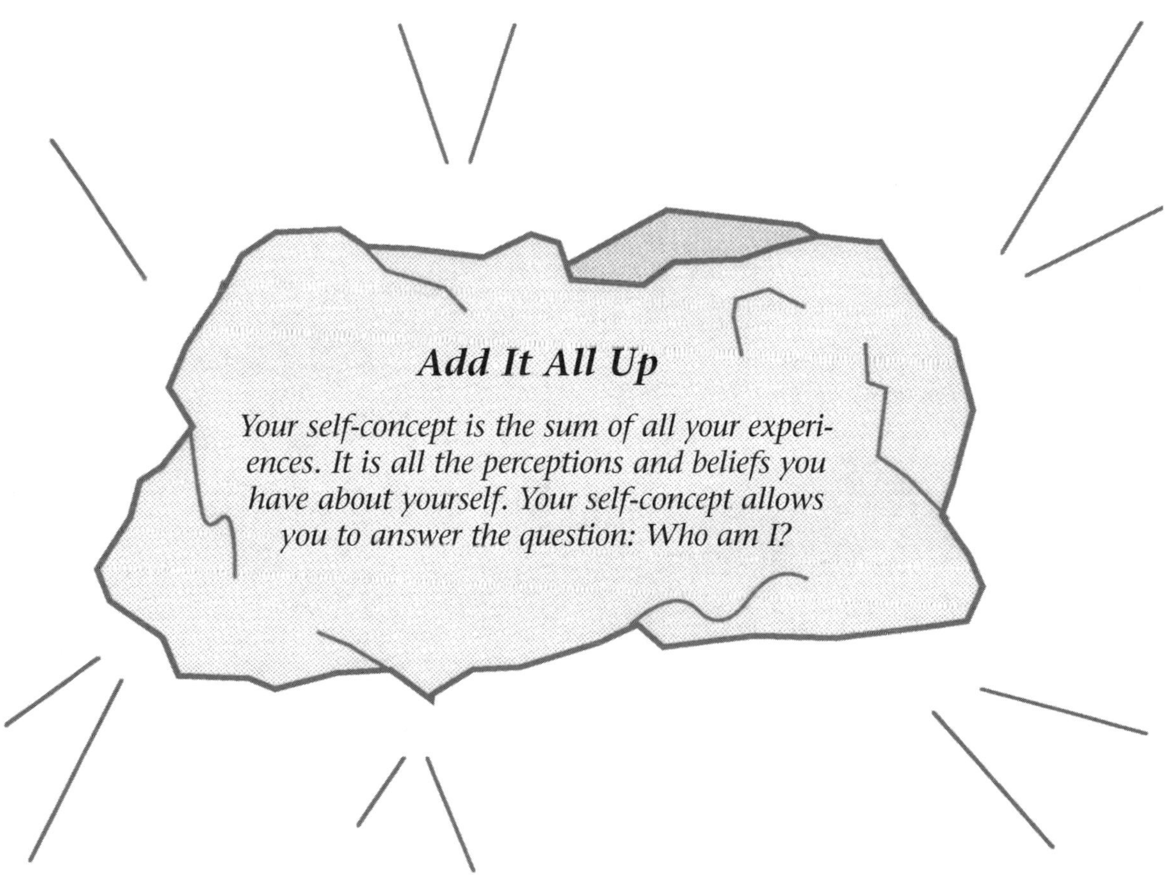

to your beliefs about friendships. Use Activity 5.4 to help you understand your self-concept.

When people are young, they bring many friendship experiences into their self-concepts. Some of these experiences are happy and some are sad. If the majority of these experiences are happy ones, it is likely that people will see themselves as being able to make friends and have enjoyable friendships. On the other hand, when people place more importance on their sad experiences, they may see themselves as not very friendly, or as unable to make friends because others have rejected them.

Sometimes young children say, "Nobody wants to be my friend." When these feelings make up their self-concepts, children might behave in unfriendly ways. Remember, the beliefs that people hold guide their behavior.

Think about yourself for a moment. Can you remember a time when a friend rejected you? Perhaps it was someone who told you that he or she was not going to be your friend anymore. If you remember an experience like that, it is probably still painful to think about it today, even though it may have happened a long time ago.

Now, think of what your life might be like if you had many painful experiences. How would you feel about forming new friendships? How much would you trust the friends you had? If you walked into a room full of people whom you did not know, how do you think you would behave? It might be difficult to make friends easily. If your past friendships had not been trustworthy, it might be hard to find new friends to trust.

As you can see, new friendships are influenced by how you have been "invited" in past friendships as well as how you have "invited" others. If people receive many positive messages about friendships, these messages are brought into their self-concepts, and as a result, they believe that they are friendly people. If on the other hand they are "disinvited" in their attempts to form friendships or they consistently reject others, then they may have negative and unfriendly feelings about themselves and others.

Sometimes friendships change. You saw an example of this earlier in the story about Naomi. Occasionally, people whom you like stop being your friends, and others whom you dislike may become new friends. You might wonder how this is so. Does your self-concept change to allow this to happen? This is a very important question, which we will now consider.

Can the Self Change?

The self-concept is not something you can see or hold. It is not a piece of luggage that you carry around by the handle. The self-concept is an *idea* of how people grow and develop. Because you cannot see it or touch it, there are many questions about the self-concept that are difficult to answer. One of these questions is whether your self-concept can change. It can, but not always easily or quickly.

Name ______________________________ Date ______________

ACTIVITY 5.4
Picture Yourself

Draw a picture of your self-concept. Use your imagination. It can be a picture of anything you choose. Show your picture to a friend or family member, and explain to that person how the picture shows your self-concept.

Just as it takes the self-concept many years to form, it may take a long time to change. This might seem confusing, because you know that you have changed your mind about many things. Friendships, for example, sometimes change very quickly. When friendships change, does the self-concept also change? Perhaps, but probably very little. Although it can change, the self-concept is fairly stable. If it were not stable, people would tend to change too often and too quickly, and their lives would be very confusing. Each person's self-concept changes slowly as the person accepts new perceptions about himself or herself, about others, and about his or her experiences.

Your perceptions of your experiences allow you to form beliefs about yourself and others. Friendships that you form are based not only on your views of certain people, but also on the beliefs that you hold about yourself and others. When you break a friendship, it may change a perception you have about a particular person, but it does not necessarily change the beliefs you have about all your other friends. For example, if you find out a very close friend has been lying to you, your opinion of that person may change and your trust in that friendship may be broken—but only for that one person, not for all people. You will still be able to trust and believe others, and they in turn will believe you. In this way, your self-concept remains fairly stable.

If people suddenly lose very close friends, their self-concepts can change. To understand how this happens, think about listening to your favorite music on the radio. When you are listening to the music and the radio is nearby, you are attentive to it—maybe even to the point of singing along. If someone comes by and turns off the radio, you notice it right away, and say, "Hey, I was listening to that!" At that point, you are saying, "This music is important to me!" Without your favorite music, there is an emptiness around you. In much the same way, you would feel bad if you lost a very close friend who was an important part of your life. There would be an emptiness that might alter some views you have of yourself and your friendships. As a result, your self-concept might change.

What would happen, however, if you were listening to your music and you got up and walked out of the room? The further away you walked, the less you would notice the music. If you went to another part of the house or outside and someone turned off the radio, you would not notice it because you were no longer hearing it. It is similar when you break up friendships that are not as important to you. Just as the music was further away from you, some friendships are further away in their importance to you. Therefore, they are easier to change without disrupting your beliefs about yourself or about other friendships. In such cases, the self-concept would not change much, if at all.

How the self-concept develops, and the facts and beliefs that make up your self-concept, all play an important role in the friendships you make. To understand this better, you must examine your *self* and your friendships a little more closely.

THE SELF AND FRIENDSHIPS

At this point you may be asking, "What does all of this self-concept stuff have to do with friendship?" This is a good question. To answer it, let us review a few things about the self-concept. First, the self consists of facts and beliefs. Facts are those features about yourself that are real. Beliefs are the ideas that you have about yourself.

Second, the self-concept is learned through many life experiences. It is learned by compiling numerous perceptions about yourself and the world around you. Perceptions that fit your beliefs about yourself are *accepted* into the self-concept, but perceptions that do not fit with your beliefs are *rejected*. If you understand about the self-concept, its parts and how it is formed, then you will have a better understand-

Gold Nugget

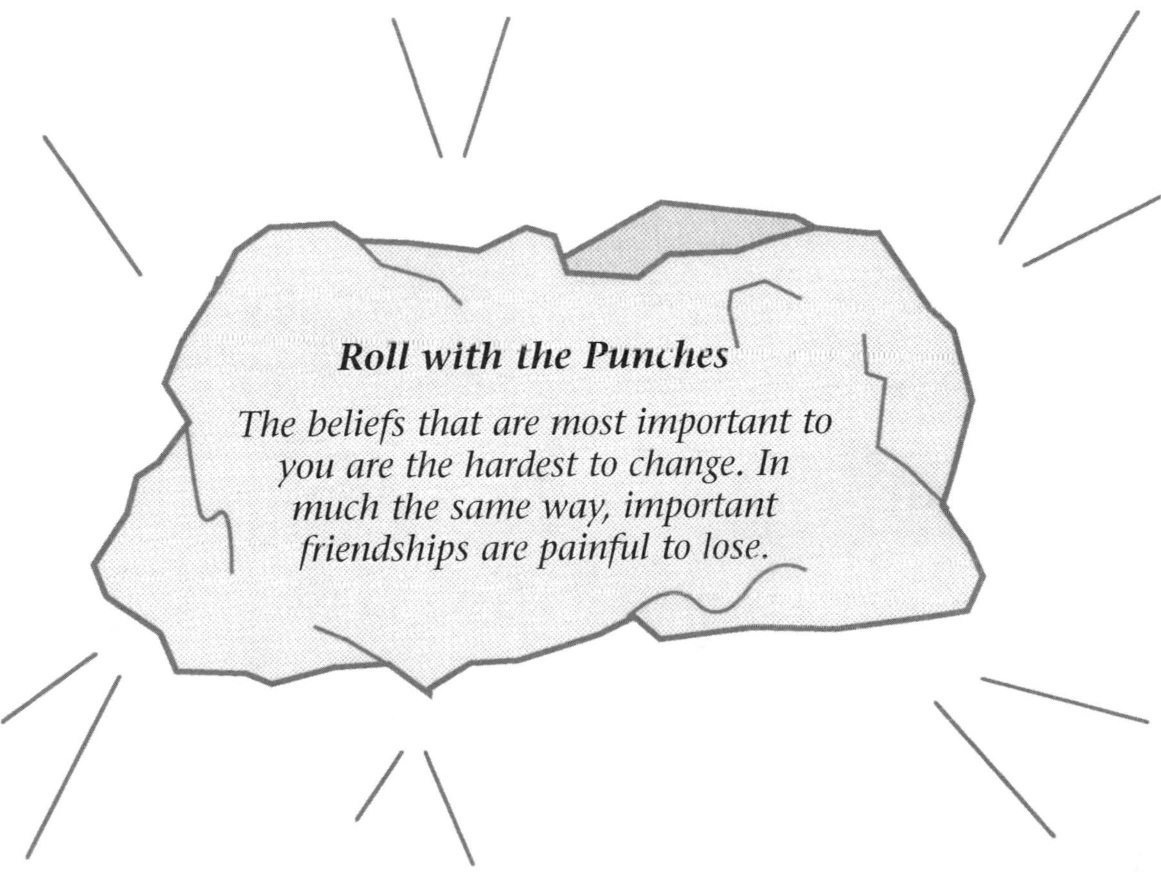

ing of the friendships you have now, and those that you will continue to make throughout your life.

Reflections of the Self

In a way, your friendships are reflections of your self-concept. The beliefs you hold about yourself and the world around you are frequently similar to the beliefs held by your friends. As you learned earlier, to some extent this is why you are friends; you tend to like the same things and agree on many issues. For example, if you really like to play sports, chances are good that your best friends like to play sports too. If you are a good student in school, your best friends are probably good students also. People become friends because they see things that they have in common with each other. In this way, your friendships validate who you think you are. Use Activity 5.5 to explore a friendship.

Sometimes you can be confused by friendships that other people have. Have you ever said something like, "How can Sally be friends with Hashim *(Pronounced HA-SHEEM)*? He's so weird!" You see Hashim in a different way than Sally sees him. She has found a way that he fits into her world, and therefore she can form a friendship with him. To do the same, you would have to examine some of the beliefs you hold and decide whether you want to change any of them. By changing some of your beliefs, you permit yourself to form a friendship with Hashim. Of course, Hashim has something to say about this too. The friendship can be formed only if both of you want it.

Changing Friendships

Because friendships mirror our self-concepts, they tend to change as our perceptions change. Think back about two years ago. How many of your close friends today were your friends two years ago? Your self-concept is developing and changing in ways that allow you to move in and out of many friendships.

There are other factors besides your self-concept that contribute to changing friendships. These include moving to a new town, changing schools, and joining new clubs or sport activities. Chances are, however, that even if you never moved, changed schools, or joined new groups, some of your friendships would still change from year to year.

Ensuring Beneficial Friendships

Knowing that your self-concept changes and contributes to your friendships raises the question, "How can you be sure that your friendships are good for you?" Everyone wants friendships that will be helpful to them. Nobody wants a "friend" who will harm him or her. How do you ensure that you have chosen good friends?

There are no guaranteed ways of knowing, but by understanding yourself, planning positive messages to send to others, and examining the messages that others

Name ______________________________ Date ______________

ACTIVITY 5.5
Self-Concept List

Make a list of seven most important things in your life. Your list might consist of people, objects, ideas, or other things. Ask a friend to make a list also. Compare your two lists and see what things are most important to each of you. What are the similarities and differences on your lists? Now cross off three things on your list, and ask your friend to do the same. Compare and talk about the items you each have left. This activity will help you get to know yourself and your friend a little better.

Seven Most Important Things

send to you, you have a good chance of choosing helpful friendships. These messages, as you have seen, are the *invitations* and *disinvitations* that you send and receive every day. Understanding how these messages contribute to the development of your self-concept is the first step in understanding how they will influence your friendships.

The Self and Invitations

Your self-concept is greatly influenced by the messages that you receive. In addition, the self-concept guides you in determining what kinds of messages to send. The more positive messages you send and receive, the more likely that you will create a positive self-concept. Likewise, when mostly negative messages enter people's self-concepts, they are likely to give negative responses in return. In this way, the relationship between positive and negative messages and the self-concept is cyclical—like a revolving door.

Revolving Door

A revolving kind of door that you sometimes see at department stores goes around in a circle, and there are compartments to fit several people in the door at one time. With a revolving door, people can go into the store through the same doorway by which others are coming out. By viewing the self-concept as having a revolving door, you could say that the types of messages that go through the door are the same types that go out.

If good and beneficial messages are sent to you and you accept them, then it is likely that you will send beneficial messages in return. On the other hand, if you always receive mean, nasty messages, then you may become a person who always sends those kinds of messages to others. More important, you will also send unkind messages to yourself.

Sadly, some people are sent very few positive messages. As a result, they have learned to accept the only messages they receive, which frequently are negative and harmful ones. The more negative they feel about themselves, the less they will be able to send positive messages. In this way, their revolving door continues spinning out of control, taking in and sending out *disinvitations*. Remember what you learned earlier about intentionality and unintentionality? Sometimes, people become unintentionally trapped in situations, like revolving doors. The longer they stay trapped, the more difficult it is for them to change things that will make a positive difference.

The longer you are trapped in a negative revolving door, the more difficult it is to get out. You keep spinning and spinning, and feel as if you are losing control. It is much the same way with your self-concept and negative beliefs. The more you believe negative things about yourself (even though some of them may be unintentional), the more likely it is that you will lose control of your positive behaviors and

Help!

Cartoon 5-B

Role Play 5-B
Treasure Hunt

Instructions: Your leader will ask you if you want to go on a treasure hunt and look for "treasured" traits about your classmates. Each student will write down one positive and one negative characteristic about himself or herself, and then write a number from 1 to 5 next to those two traits.

Next, you will all write headings for two columns on your papers. One column heading is *Positive,* the other is *Negative*. When every student has written two characteristics and assigned numbers to each, and all of you have written the two column headings on a piece of paper, the role play begins.

You will all walk around the room and ask each other for a certain number. For example, one student would approach another and say, "Do you have a number 2?" If the second student has not numbered either characteristic as 2, that student says, "Sorry, I have no number 2," and the first student moves on to another student. If the second student says, "Yes, and it is friendly" or some other positive characteristic, that means the number was correct and the characteristic was "friendly." The first student writes down the characteristic on his or her list under the *Positive*: heading and moves on.

When a student guesses a correct number, but the second student gives a negative characteristic, the receiving student must write that trait down in the *Negative* column. The first student who collects five more positive characteristics than negative characteristics yells, "I found the treasure!"

begin behaving in negative ways, sending intentional disinvitations to everyone around you.

It is important to learn how to help yourself out of negative situations. To do so, you must control the revolving door of your self-concept. One way to gain control is by learning to invite yourself.

Inviting the Self

From time to time, we all get caught in a revolving door that sends us negative messages. You know this is happening when you begin to put yourself down and say things like, "I am stupid. No wonder nobody wants to be my friend." Interestingly, the more negative you feel about yourself, the less likely that others will want to invite you. No one wants to be friends with a grump!

It is important to learn how to send inviting messages to yourself. By doing good things for yourself, you maintain confidence, and this gives you an optimistic stance, which, in turn, helps you make friends. A wise lesson is that friendship begins at home, with yourself. If you invite yourself, you are in the best position to be invited by others. In contrast, if you always disinvite yourself, you are likely to be disinvited, or at best ignored, by others. Activity 5.6 will help you look at ways to be *invited* and to be *inviting*.

Positive messages are powerful ingredients for forming a healthy self-concept and in developing beneficial friendships. How do you send positive messages? In the next section, you will learn about the ways you invite yourself and others.

Gold Nugget

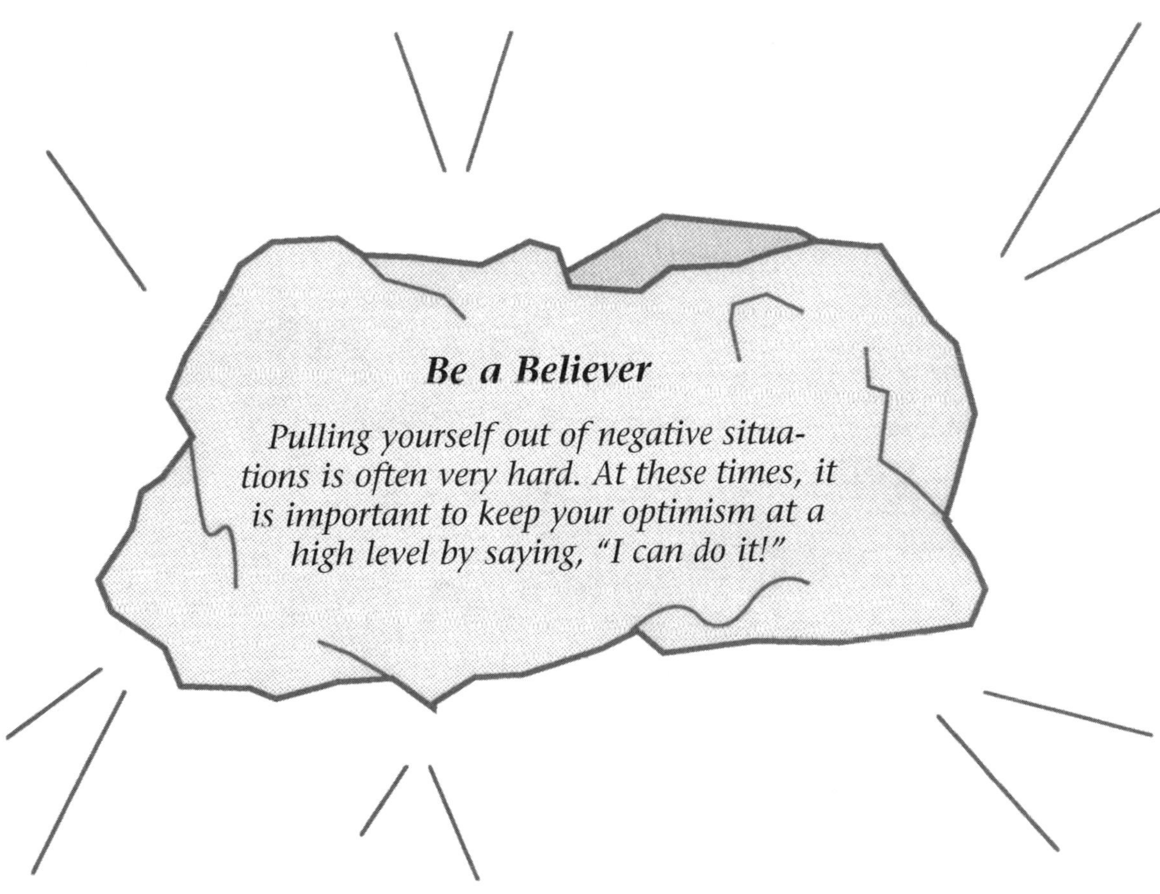

Name ______________________ Date ______________

ACTIVITY 5.6
Friendship Résumé

A résumé is a description of yourself that you prepare when looking for a job. Employers read your résumé, and decide whether to interview you. Prepare a résumé of yourself as if you were applying for a friendship. List your positive qualities and experiences. Decide what to put on your résumé to attract helpful friendships for yourself.

My Friendship Résumé

Section 6

CREATING INVITATIONS TO FRIENDSHIP

GROUP LEADER INSTRUCTIONS

Summary:

This section outlines the steps used in an inviting process. Simply put, it teaches students "how to invite." Included in this process are the following six steps: (1) wanting to, (2) creating the invitation, (3) sending the invitation, (4) checking for reception, (5) negotiating change, and (6) measuring up.

In the part of this section about creating invitations, students are reintroduced to the power of perceptions when they learn about *reading the situation* and *setting the stage* for successful invitations.

Objectives

1. To learn about the process of creating and sending positive messages.
2. To understand how perceptions can influence the success or failure of messages we send to others.
3. To learn about negotiating differences and altering one's messages so they are more successful.

Activities

Activity 6.1 is a creative endeavor that asks students to draw and color an invitation. By sharing their drawings with each other, students can compare and contrast their pictures and the colors that they used to depict an invitation. The rationale for this activity is to lend some degree of concreteness to an abstract concept like "invitation."

MATERIALS

- ❒ Copies of Activity 6.1
- ❒ Pens, pencils, crayons, and other art media

Activity 6.2 asks students to think of examples of how people misread situations. Have the students read the examples of misreading situations given in this part of the section. Ask students to write their own examples (in small groups, pairs, or individually). This activity reinforces the idea of misreading situations and helps students understand how "misreads" can cause them problems with friends.

MATERIALS

- ❒ Copies of Activity 6.2
- ❒ Pencils or pens
- ❒ Chart paper or chalkboard for large group sharing

Activity 6.3 focuses on *setting the stage* when creating invitations. It asks students to make up an invitation and then list everything they would have to do to make sure their invitation was successful. It might be helpful to do this activity as a whole class first and then ask students to do it again in small groups or individually. The activity reinforces the importance of planning in creating successful invitations and emphasizes the sender's responsibility.

MATERIALS

- ❒ Copies of Activity 6.3
- ❒ Pencils or pens
- ❒ An example of an invitation for the class to do as a large group

Activity 6.4 continues application of *reading the situation* and *setting the stage*. By practicing these examples, students will become more comfortable and skilled at creating invitations.

Materials

- ❒ Copies of Activity 6.4
- ❒ Pens or pencils,

Activity 6.5 instructs students to read the story of Elmo and identify how the steps of inviting occurred in the story. This activity allows students an opportunity to demonstrate their understanding of the six steps of inviting.

Materials

- ❒ Copies of Activity 6.5
- ❒ Pens or pencils

Activity 6.6 invites students to create a personal invitation for themselves. This activity helps students to think about the six steps of inviting and what they would need to do in creating, sending, and evaluating an invitation to themselves.

Materials

- ❒ Copies of Activity 6.6
- ❒ Pens or pencils

Role Play

Role Play 6-A asks two students to act out an invitation. The other class members observe the role play and identify the steps used.

Vocabulary Words

These words may need additional explanation by the group leader, depending on the reading level of students in the class. Words with an asterisk denote concepts that may need explanation.

relatively
complex
frustrating
observant*
flourish
negotiating*
obvious
consistently
apparent
appropriate
misreadings*
sufficient
shrugged
reception*

CREATING INVITATIONS TO FRIENDSHIP

Do all the good you can, By all the means you can,
In all the ways you can, In all the places you can,
At all the times you can, to all the people you can,
As long as ever you can.

John Wesley

In the first five sections, you learned about friendship, about invitations and disinvitations, and about your self-concept. This section takes the knowledge you have gained from these earlier lessons and helps you use it. You will now learn about the process of sending positive messages and how that process can help you choose, form, and keep friendships. This section will focus on the questions of how, when, and whom to invite.

How to Invite

Learning how to invite is relatively simple, yet being consistently inviting is a challenge. This may sound like a puzzle, but it is true. Learning the steps of the inviting process is not very hard; however, putting the process to use every day is difficult. Sometimes things that look simple can be very complex. For example, you might watch a golfer on television hit a ball, and see it fly through the air with apparent ease. If you have ever tried to hit a golf ball, however, you know that it looks a lot easier than it is. Learning the basics of a golf swing is simple, but swinging consistently so that every ball you hit takes off in the right direction is another story.

Things that appear simple to one person may seem quite different to others. If we return to the example of a golf swing, we probably will find people who have learned to play golf with little effort or instruction. To them, hitting a golf ball is relatively easy, while for other people it remains a hard, frustrating task. Certainly their individual talents contribute to this difference, but as you learned earlier, human perception plays a role in how people view similar events differently. Knowing that people see golf differently helps explain in some measure their different evaluations of how difficult it is to hit a golf ball. Similarly, understanding that people have different perceptions is important when deciding what friendship messages to send. Learning about the steps of the inviting process will help you send the most successful messages.

The Process

Creating an invitation is much like assembling a model plane or baking a cake. There are steps to follow, and to be successful you want to be sure that no step is left out.

Wanting to

The first step of the inviting process is *wanting to* invite yourself or others. It sounds simple, doesn't it? Sometimes it is simple because you really want to do something, or you really want to be with someone. At other times, it is more difficult to want to invite because you are unsure of the situation or the people around you. For example, if someone asks you to go water skiing and you have never water skied before, you might hesitate because you are uncertain about it. You would not be sure that you want to accept. If after reviewing the situation, you realize that the risk is not too great and you would like a new experience of learning how to ski on water, then you might want to. It is this *wanting to* that enables you to accept an invitation.

The above example shows how wanting to plays a role when you *accept* friendly messages. Wanting to also plays a part when you *send* messages. Return to the above example and you will see how this is so. The friends who asked you to go water skiing wanted to have you with them to enjoy the fun together. If they had not wanted to be with you, they would not have asked you to go. In this way, *wanting to* plays an important role in developing friendships. You have to want to send and accept invitations if you are going to have friendships.

Inviting can look simple, but it may be difficult to do. Wanting to may seem simple, but there are many reasons why it might be hard to want to invite yourself or another person. One reason people do not invite themselves or others is that they do not think they can. They lack the optimism to make it happen. If they would say, "I can" instead of "I can't," they maintain a level of optimism that is part of *wanting to*.

Have you ever wanted to do something, but decided not to do it because you did not feel that you were able? You may have said, "I can't do that!" When people are unsure or scared about doing something new, they are quick to excuse themselves with the "I can't" pronouncement. In these cases, people might really want to, but their feelings about what others might think block them from going ahead and trying it. What people mean when they say, "I can't," is "I'm afraid," or simply, "I

Oops!
Cartoon 6-A

Gold Nugget

Be a Genie

Wishing for good things to occur works only if you take action to make good things happen.

won't do it." People also say "I can't" to themselves. This is negative self-talk that gives them an excuse for not trying something. You will learn more about self-talk later in this program.

Having the desire to invite yourself and others, and acting on this desire, are necessary parts of the first step in the inviting process. Only when you want to do things, and you behave accordingly, will you be able to move to the second step of choosing appropriate messages to send. This next step is called *creating the invitation*.

Creating the Invitation

Once you have decided that you want to do something for yourself or with other people, the next step is to design and create the message that is needed to carry out your desires. Having the desire leads to creating the invitation (Activity 6.1).

Name ______________________________ Date ______________

ACTIVITY 6.1
Draw an Invitation

Draw or paint a picture of an invitation. Let your imagination go. What is in your picture? What colors did you use? Show your picture to others, and ask them to guess what it is.

In this step, you decide what you want to have happen for yourself or others. Once that decision is made, you proceed with the creation of an appropriate invitation. Creating an invitation requires answers to a few simple questions:

1. Whom do you want to invite?
2. What invitation do you want to send?
3. When do you want to invite them?

To answer these questions, you may need some additional information in creating your invitations. In particular, you may need to know more about the person to whom you plan to send the invitation. Obtaining more information is called *reading the situation*, and having an accurate reading enables you to plan a successful message. For this reason, creating an invitation requires that you do two things: read the situation and set the stage.

Reading the situation. To invite appropriately you have to know who it is you are planning to invite. If you are going to ask other people to do something with you, you must know them well enough to know their likes, dislikes, needs, and desires. To acquire this knowledge about people, you have to *read the situation*, which means you must be observant and learn about the people with whom you want to be friends. Use Activity 6.2 to explore *misreadings*.

As an example, think about having a surprise party. Suppose you decided to throw a surprise birthday party for a friend. You planned the party, invited many people whom your friend enjoyed, and kept the secret until the lights were turned on and your friend was caught in surprise. Unfortunately, even though you planned a good party, you did not know that your friend hates surprises. Because you did not "read the situation" by taking time to learn how your friend feels about being surprised, the party became a disinviting experience for both you and your friend.

Some other examples of misreading situations and sending inappropriate messages are:

- Giving candy to a friend whose dentist has instructed him or her to stay away from sweets
- Asking new people to join an outing without first checking with the rest of your group
- Offering ice cream to someone who is trying to lose weight
- Helping yourself to a supply of paper in the classroom before checking with the teacher

Reading the situation increases the likelihood that appropriate messages can be created and sent. To create the most beneficial message, preparations need to be made and the stage needs to be set.

Name ________________________________ Date ________________

ACTIVITY 6.2
Misreadings

Think of examples of how people might misread situations. Make a list and share them with the class. After each student in the class has shared, count those that are similar. What are some of the most common *misreadings*?

Setting the stage. Having the necessary information to create an invitation leads you to the phase called *setting the stage*. Return to the example of a surprise party, and you will see what this phase is all about.

Assume that you have read the situation properly and you know that your friend loves surprises. The next step in creating an appropriate invitation would include planning the party, inviting the guests, buying refreshments, choosing the location, and *inventing* a story that will get your friend unknowingly to the party. All of these events help to *set the stage* for a successful surprise (see Activity 6.3).

Every invitation requires you to set the stage. Even when you send an invitation that requires little thought or planning, you still want the message to be successful, and that means being sure it is appropriate for the person, time, and place. This is what reading the situation and setting the stage are all about—being sure that the messages you create and send are right for the people, places, and times that you intended. Activity 6.4 helps you practice reading the situation and setting the stage. When you have decided that the situation is right and the stage is set, then you can proceed to the next step and send the invitation.

Sending the Invitation

It may seem silly to have a step called "sending the invitation" because you think that if it is not sent, then it is not an invitation. This is true. Frequently you hear people say, "I've been meaning to invite you over." By making such statements, people are saying that they have "wanted to" invite, and may have even "created" an invitation, but never have gotten around to sending it. To be received, messages must first be sent.

There are many reasons why people do not send the friendly messages that they have created. Sometimes they forget. For example, you might be saving money for an important purchase, and each week you intend to put a dollar in your bank. However, a couple of times you forget to put money in the bank, and when the time comes to make the purchase, you are short the amount of money that you need. You forgot to send yourself the necessary *invitations* to acquire sufficient funds.

People's feelings also can block them from sending invitations. It takes courage to invite yourself and others. If you are thinking about doing something new, difficult, or risky, such as singing for a show, entering a science fair, or learning how to play golf, you will need courage to send yourself the invitation. Likewise, when you send invitations to others, you face the risk of being turned down, and that takes courage as well.

Sending invitations can be risky, but it is wise to take such risks. If you are going to form friendships, inviting messages will have to be created and sent. People who fail to invite themselves and others cannot be expected to develop many friendships. This is seen in a story about a teenage boy who was new to the neighborhood.

Name ______________________ Date ____________

ACTIVITY 6.3
Setting the Stage

Make up an invitation you would like to send to someone. List below everything you would have to plan and do to make this invitation successful.

The invitation is: ______________________

I would set the stage by: ______________________

Name ______________________ Date ______________

ACTIVITY 6.4
Reading and Setting Practice

What would you have to do to read the situation and set the stage for the following invitations?

1. Inviting a friend to have dinner at your house: ______________________

2. Asking a friend if she or he wants some of your candy bar: ______________________

3. Inviting a classmate to play kickball: ______________________

4. Taking your new puppy over to a neighbor's house: ______________________

Gold Nugget

NEW IN THE NEIGHBORHOOD

The boy wanted to find some friends, but every time he thought about going over to the houses of neighborhood teens who lived on his street, he would decide not to go. He was unsure about how the others would treat him. As a result, the boy became unhappy with his new home, and complained to his parents that there was nothing to do and nobody liked him. He would say to his mother, "I don't like this town because I have no friends." Fortunately, there was a girl in his neighborhood who had the courage to go over to the new boy's house and introduce herself. From that invitation the two became friends and the new boy was introduced to other teenagers in the neighborhood.

Sending messages is an important step. An invitation that is never sent is not an invitation; it is just a good idea. Sending a positive message, however, does not complete the process. There is another step: to be sure the message you send is also received.

Checking for Reception

Sometimes messages are sent but never received. Have you ever heard of letters getting lost in the mail? The same can be said for invitations. People with good intentions sometimes send messages that are never received by the other party. This happens most frequently because of *miscommunications*. It is a big word—*miscommunications*, but this is often the reason friendships never happen, or even worse, why some friendships end unhappily.

Miscommunications are messages and signals that are misunderstood, not heard, or never received by the people for whom you intended them. It is not only important to send invitations, but also to check and be sure that the invitations have been received. The following story shows what can happen when messages are sent but not checked for reception.

CLASS PROJECT

Robin, an eighth-grade student, was assigned a team project for social studies with three other students in her class. The class projects focused on Asia, the continent the class was studying. Robin and her group decided to build a model of the Great Wall of China as their project. The other students in Robin's group, Bernice, Gustav (*Pronounced GOO-STAHV*), and Hector, decided to meet at Gustav's house after school to begin planning the project. Robin was at the Media Center when they decided, so they put a note on her desk telling her to meet them at Gustav's house. While Robin was gone, another student accidentally bumped her desk and the note fell unnoticed to the floor. When Robin returned to the class she never saw the note. As a result she did not meet Bernice, Gustav, and Hector to plan the project.

Robin's classmates were upset with her. They thought she did not meet with them because she wanted them to do all the planning. When Bernice, Gustav, and Hector arrived at school the next day, they complained to Robin. Even when she explained that she never saw the note, they were not too sure she was telling the truth. This miscommunication, simply caused by a lost note, led to anger and distrust in their relationship. If her friends had checked to be sure that Robin had read their note, none of these feelings would have dampened their relationship or hindered work on their project.

On occasion, invitations are sent and received, but not accepted. When this happens, the person who sends the message must find out why it has not been accepted. If changes can be made to make the message more acceptable, then the sender has the responsibility for making those changes. This involves the next step of the inviting process—negotiating change.

Negotiating Change

Not all invitations are accepted. Sometimes people cannot accept a message because they either already have other plans, cannot afford to accept, are unsure about it, or need more information. When this happens, it is best to find out what can be changed about the message to make it more acceptable.

Perhaps a different time or place might be considered for the invitation to be accepted. For example, if you ask a friend over for dinner but the friend's family has already made plans for the evening, maybe another time could be offered for the dinner invitation. Usually you can tell that a person wants to negotiate another invitation if he or she says, "Maybe we could do it another time," or something similar.

By offering to change or adjust an invitation to make it more acceptable, you allow the door to friendship to remain open. When you are flexible with the messages you send to others, your friends respect your willingness to create messages that fit their situations. In Section 4, you learned that people accept only things that fit into

Gold Nugget

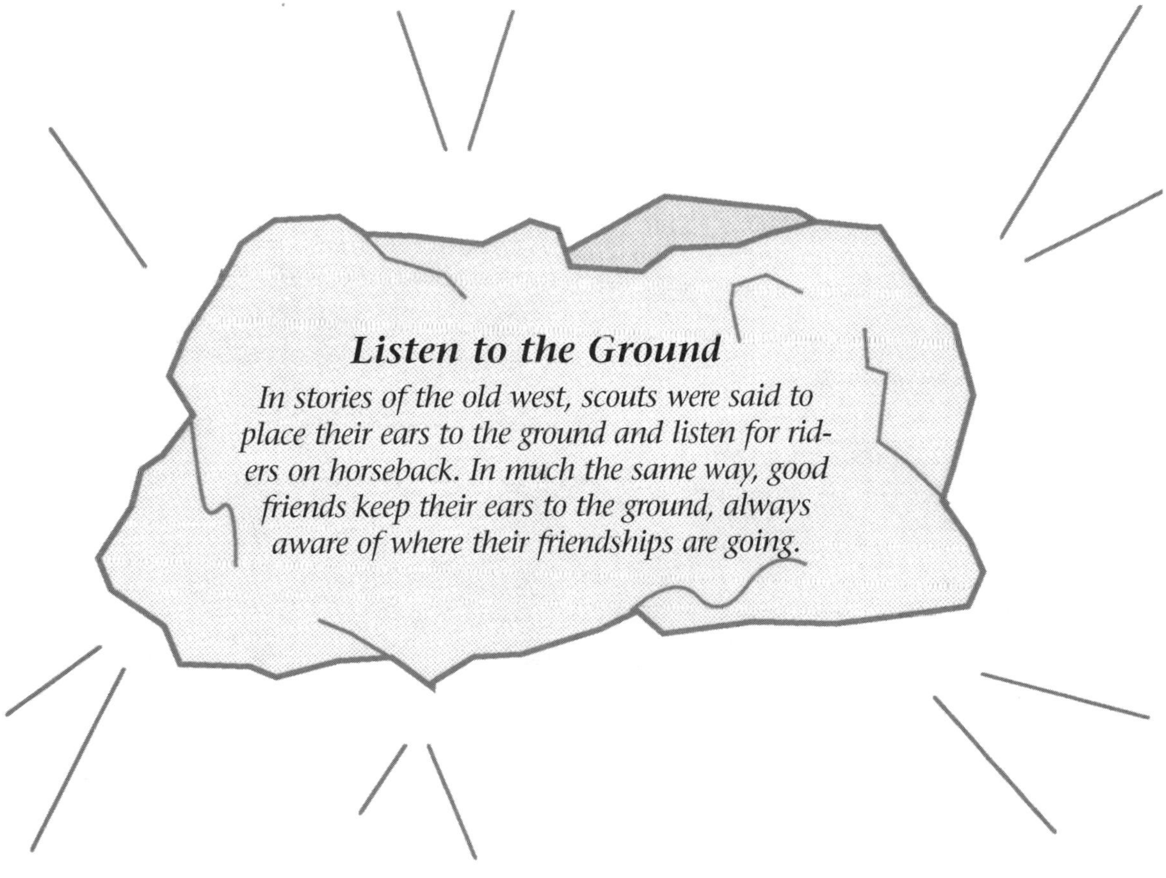

their world as they see it. Your willingness to adjust your messages to fit into a friend's world will usually be warmly accepted and will help you make more friends. Having your invitations accepted leads to the last step of the inviting process. In the final step, you evaluate the result of your invitations. This is called *measuring up*.

Measuring Up

An invitation should provide a happy, joyful, exciting, learning, or other beneficial experience for you and those to whom you send it. In sum, the invitation should measure up to your expectations. To check your success in creating and sending invitations, you want to measure how beneficial they are for yourself and your friends.

Measuring up simply means checking to see that everything has gone according to plan and that everyone has benefited from the invitation. Sometimes positive outcomes are obvious because people express their pleasure openly. For example, if you invite a friend to spend the night and together you play games, watch television, laugh at funny stories, and enjoy each other's company, it is easy to see that your invitation has been successful.

At other times, it is more difficult to measure the outcome of an invitation. This is particularly true when the results of an invitation will not be seen for a long time. An example of this can be seen in the story of Elmo—a boy who had much trouble in school.

ELMO

One day Elmo was sent to the principal's office for misbehaving in class. While talking with him, the principal noticed that Elmo kept looking at all the live green plants in the office. He said, "Do you like plants, Elmo?" Elmo shrugged, "I don't know, I've never had a plant." The principal invited Elmo to choose any plant in the office. He asked only that Elmo be sure to take care of the plant, so that it would live and grow. Elmo chose a plant and the principal taught him how to care for it.

One of the immediate results of this invitation by the principal was that he and Elmo became friends, and their friendship helped Elmo behave better in school. Another result, however, was not noticed for several years. During his senior year in high school, Elmo decided he wanted to continue his studies in college and major in botany.

Do you know what botany is? That is right! It is the study of plant life! The story of Elmo illustrates all the steps of the inviting process: wanting to, creating, sending, checking reception, negotiating, and measuring up. Each step of the process is important to the development of your friendships. And remember, the first invitation begins with *you*. Look at the steps of inviting in Activity 6.5.

Name ______________________ Date ______________

ACTIVITY 6.5
The Steps of Elmo's Invitation

Answer the following questions to see how the steps of inviting occurred in the story of Elmo.

1. How did the principal show that he *wanted to* invite Elmo? ______________

2. What did Elmo do to show that he *wanted to* accept the principal's invitation? ______________

3. In creating the invitation, what did the principal do to *read the situation* and *set the stage*?

4. How did the principal send the invitation and *check reception*? ______________

5. Was there any negotiation? If so, what was it? ______________

6. If you were Elmo, how would you measure the success of this invitation? ______________

Role Play 6-A
The Invitation

Instructions: Your group leader will ask two students, a boy and a girl, to volunteer for the role play, and then give them a few minutes to read their respective parts. When they are ready, they will begin the role play in front of the class. Each class member will have a copy of the Class Observation Sheet. As the role play continues, class members will be asked to identify who was the sender and who was the receiver of the invitation. Also, the class should listen for clues that identify the steps that are processed during the role-play. As you discuss these steps, your leader will ask you for examples of *reading the situation* and *setting the stage* that you observed during the role play.

Male Student: *(approaches the girl)* Hi, (girl's name).

Female Student: Hi, (boy's name). What are you doing here after school?

Male Student: I asked my mother to pick me up later because I wanted to ask you something.

Female Student: What were you going to ask me?

Male Student: Well, the city is having a tennis tournament at the end of next month and it will include mixed doubles matches. I want to play singles, but I also want to play doubles if I can get a partner. I have seen you playing tennis sometimes after school—hitting a ball against the wall or playing with other girls. Do you like to play tennis?

Female Student: Yes, but I'm not very good. What's a mixed doubles match?

Male Student: Mixed doubles is when a boy and girl play as a team against another boy and girl. I have watched you hit tennis balls, and you are good. Do you know how to keep score?

Female Student: Of course I do! I'm not stupid!

Male Student: I'm sorry; didn't mean to insult you. Have you ever played in a tournament?

Female Student: No. I have only played with my friends and family. My mom plays tennis and is really good. She has taught me how to play. She plays in tournaments.

Male Student: I played singles in the city tournament last year. It was fun. After the tournament, there is a cookout for players and their families and the trophies are given out.

Female Student: Did you win a trophy last year?

Male Student: No, but it was still a lot of fun. I would like to play both singles and mixed doubles this time. If I do, would you be my doubles partner?

Female Student: Me? You want me to be your partner? Wow, I don't know if I could.

Male Student: Why not? Won't you be here at the end of the month?

Female Student: Oh yes, I'll be here, but I'm not sure I'm good enough to play in a tournament.

Male Student: Well, I have watched you play, and you're as good or better than most of the girls in last year's tournament. Heck, you're better than most of the boys!

Female Student: I don't know.

Male Student: How about if you and I stay after school tomorrow and we'll hit with each other? That way, you will see me play and can decide if you want to be partners.

Female Student: I can do that. Yeah, let's play tomorrow. Then you'll see how *bad* I really am! I'll check with my mother, and call you tonight to let you know for sure.

Male Student: Thanks, (Girl's name). I'll wait for your call. Hope you can play. I think we'll make a good team.

In finishing this section about the inviting process, it is appropriate to use the steps of the process and create an invitation. Activity 6.6 asks you to do this. Start with an invitation to yourself, and then use the steps to create invitations to send to others.

Name ______________________ Date ____________

Role Play 6-A
The Invitation

Class Observation Sheet

1. Who was the sender? ______________________
2. Who was the receiver? ______________________
3. What did you see or hear during:
   a. Wanting to ______________________
   b. Creating the Invitation ______________________
   c. Sending the Invitation ______________________
   d. Checking for Reception ______________________
   e. Negotiating Change ______________________

Name ______________________________ Date ______________

ACTIVITY 6.6
Follow the Steps

Use the steps of the inviting process to send an invitation to yourself. Think of what you want to do for yourself, create the invitation, send it, accept it, and evaluate it. After you have been successful with yourself, use the steps to invite a friend.

My Personal Invitation: ______________________________

Things I need to do to send myself this invitation:

Section 7

MAKING CHOICES AND RESOLVING DIFFERENCES

GROUP LEADER INSTRUCTIONS

Summary:

This section examines four choices that students make when inviting friends. The first two choices involve whether to send or not send a particular message. The second choices pertain to receiving messages and ask students to decide whether to accept or not accept another person's message.

The second part of the section asks students to consider what happens to friendships when there are differences and disagreements. Here, students will learn how the invitational approach can help them handle conflicts with their friends. You may want to introduce other conflict resolution models in this section and have the students evaluate these models from an invitational viewpoint.

The final part of Section 7 asks students to think about whom they want to send positive messages to. It begins with "themselves" and mentions family, friends, and others.

Objectives

1. To learn about the choices one faces in sending and receiving friendship messages.
2. To explore positive ways of dealing with differences and disagreements with friends.
3. To appreciate the importance of inviting oneself in order to be successful in inviting others.

Activities

Activity 7.1 asks students to think of times when it might be best *not* to send an inviting message. This activity emphasizes the importance of accepting the perceptions of others and reading situations carefully before inviting friendships.

MATERIALS

- ❒ Copies of Activity 7.1
- ❒ Pens and pencils
- ❒ Chart paper or chalkboard to record class responses

Activity 7.2 has students recall a time when they decided to do something, but it did not work out very well. Students are asked about their feelings at the time, and what they would do differently if they could do it over again. This activity helps students explore elements that may lead them *not* to accept certain messages.

MATERIALS

- ❒ Copies of Activity 7.2
- ❒ Pencils or pens
- ❒ Chart paper or chalkboard for large group discussion

Activity 7.3 asks students to read five descriptions of *obstacles to listening* and rate themselves on these obstacles. After students have read the obstacles and rated themselves, ask them to share their self-ratings either in a small group or with the class. Hold a class discussion to help students learn how to avoid these obstacles to listening.

MATERIALS

- ❒ Copies of Activity 7.3
- ❒ Pens or pencils

Activity 7.4 asks students to keep track of all the invitations they send and receive during a period of time. This activity can be done as a homework assignment. By tracking the messages they send and receive, students monitor their own positive behaviors and evaluate the number and quality of positive messages they receive from others.

MATERIALS

- ❒ Copies of Activity 7.4
- ❒ Pencils or pens

Activity 7.5 asks students to design a "want ad" to search for a new friend. Encourage students to be creative by showing them samples of want ads from the newspaper. By designing a want ad for a friend, students highlight those qualities and values that are important to them.

MATERIALS

- ❒ Copies of Activity 7.5
- ❒ Drawing paper
- ❒ Pens, pencils, crayons, or other art media

Activity 7.6 asks students to write their own "Gold Nugget." This activity encourages students to think about an axiom of their own making. By writing one of their own, students will reflect on an idea about friendship that is important to them.

MATERIALS

- ❒ Copies of Activity 7.6
- ❒ Pens or pencils

ROLE PLAY

Role Play 7-A asks three students to act out a disagreement among friends about what position each will play in a baseball game. The class observes the role play and decides which friend used an *inviting* approach to resolve the conflict.

Role Play 7-B asks two students to act out a discussion between two friends. The class observes the role play and discusses the listening skills used by the two friends.

Role Play 7-C asks five students to go outside the classroom. The teacher or group leader calls in the first student and tells that student about an event. The second student is invited in, and the first student repeats the event to the second student. Then the third student is invited back to class and the second student reports the event to the third, and so forth, until the fifth student comes back and hears the message. After the role play, the teacher or group leader leads the class in a discussion about listening and how stories can change.

Vocabulary Words

These words may need additional explanation by the group leader depending on the reading level of students in the class. Words with an asterisk denote concepts that may need explanation.

narrowed down*
persistent*
appropriateness*
element
feud
obvious
persevere*
nonacceptance*
determining
convenient
resolving
combative*
illustration
alternatives

MAKING CHOICES AND RESOLVING DIFFERENCES

The language of Friendship is not words but meaning.

Henry David Thoreau

Now that you have learned the steps of inviting, it is time to learn about when to send messages and when not to send them. When people think about sending positive messages to themselves and others, there are choices to be made. These choices can be narrowed down to four possibilities: when to send, when not to send, when to accept, and when not to accept.

This may seem like a riddle, but it is not. You have already learned that sending an invitation is very important. Now you will learn that a second, and equally important, choice is *not sending* an invitation. In addition to these two choices about sending friendly messages, you also have two choices to make when you receive messages: *to accept* or *not to accept*. Let us first explore the choice of sending one more time.

SENDING

Earlier, you learned that to be an invitation, a message must be sent. Positive messages cannot be realized by your friends if you never send them. Having the desire and creating an invitation in your mind do little to develop friendships. Your invitations must be delivered and received if friendships are to be formed.

You have learned that it takes courage to send invitations because sometimes they are not accepted. When this happens, you may wonder why, and you may even feel rejected. It will help you to have the courage to send invitations if you remember these points:

1. Not all invitations can be accepted. Sometimes people cannot accept because they do not have the time, or part of the invitation does not suit them.

2. Nonacceptance of an invitation does not mean that you are rejected. Sometimes people honestly cannot accept, but they very much want you to invite them again at another time, or in a different way.
3. Some people have a difficult time accepting any type of invitation. There are people who repeatedly tell you that they "just can't accept" your invitation. While it will be difficult, you must be persistent. If you really want to be friends, keep trying. Look for just the right invitation, and if you persist gently with people's best interest in mind, someday you may be successful in having your invitation accepted. When you do, you may win a good friend for life!
4. When in doubt, send. If you have created a message that you are certain your friend will like, but you are uncertain your friend will accept, send it. It is best to send something for your friend to consider than to have it stay in your back pocket! Sending the message allows the opportunity for you and your friend to negotiate any changes so that a new invitation can be created, sent, and accepted.

Not Sending

Although it is true that an invitation must be sent, remember that perception, a person's point of view, plays an important role in determining what is inviting and what is disinviting. Sometimes people create messages that they think are positive, but the people who receive the messages look at them quite differently. Usually this happens when people who send the messages do not take the time to read the situation.

When you are unsure about the appropriateness of a message, it may be best not to send it. For example, you go over to a friend's house to ask her to play softball, but because she is studying for a math test, you decide to ask her at a more convenient time. Use Activity 7.1 to think of times when it's best not to send an invitation.

As you can see, sending and not sending are two choices people make when they think about inviting themselves or others. In the same way, people who receive messages must decide to accept or not accept.

Accepting

Receiving invitations is wonderful, but it is not without responsibility. The first responsibility is to decide whether the invitation can and should be accepted. Can you think of times that people invited you, and you thought about whether or not

Name ______________________________ Date ______________

ACTIVITY 7.1
When Not to Send

Think of examples where it may be best for you not to send an inviting message. Write down at least one example, and share it in class. See if other students agree that the time was not right to send your invitation.

Example: ____

to accept? Some questions you might have asked yourself when thinking about these messages are:

1. Is this going to be good for me?
2. Will my parents let me?
3. Do I have the time to do this?
4. Is this going to be dangerous ?
5. Is it against the rules?
6. Will I be scared?
7. Do I want to be with this person?

Accepting invitations requires some of the same conditions that sending does. It requires courage because when you say yes, you trust that people's intentions are honest and that they will follow through with their messages. The courage to accept an invitation is related to the element of trust, which you have learned is so necessary in forming and keeping friendships. When you accept an invitation, you place your trust in the person who has sent it

Trusting the sender is particularly important when you are uncertain about the message you have received. If you trust the sender, the same rule that applies to sending messages also applies to accepting them: *When in doubt, accept.* Of course, the opposite is also true. If you do not trust the sender and you doubt the appropriateness of a message, it may be best *not to accept.* This brings us to the last of the four choices.

Not Accepting

At times, the best thing you can do is not accept an invitation. Just as there are times when it is best not to send an invitation, it is also right for you not to accept some of the messages you receive. Accepting something from someone when you know it is not his or hers to give, joining friends after school when your family is expecting you home, and hanging out with a group that usually gets into trouble are a few examples of messages that should be reconsidered, and probably not accepted. Use Activity 7.2 to examine invitations that it's best not to accept.

When you are trying to establish new friendships, it is difficult not to accept friendly messages, yet messages that jeopardize other friendships or family trust should not be accepted. Accepting them is disinviting to yourself and others.

The ideas of sending, not sending, accepting, and not accepting are useful when considering disinvitations as well as invitations. This is particularly true when you have disagreements with your friends and you are choosing messages to send, or deciding which ones not to send them during this disagreement. The messages you choose can either help to resolve differences or fuel the disagreement.

Name ______________________ Date ______________

ACTIVITY 7.2
Invitations Not to Accept

Think of an invitation that you accepted once, but that did not turn out very well. Write down the invitation, and answer the questions that follow. Share your answers with your classmates.

An Unsuccessful Invitation: ______________________

____

____

____

____

Questions:

When you accepted the invitation, did you feel good about it? ______________________

____

____

____

____

Was the invitation sent by someone you knew and trusted? ______________________

____

____

____

____

What made the invitation turn out badly? ______________________

____

____

____

____

What would you do differently if you could do it over again? ______________________

____

____

____

____

RESOLVING DIFFERENCES

Differences and disagreements are common among friends. Unfortunately, when some people have differences, what sometimes begins as a minor misunderstanding turns into a major feud. Usually, this happens because they choose to argue and fight rather than to listen to each other's point of view and resolve the disagreement.

Think of a time when you and a friend had an argument. What happened? What type of messages did you send to your friend during this argument? Did you send a message of listening and resolving differences, or was it a message of arguing and fighting? If you decided to send combative messages, or if you accepted a challenge to fight, then you may have become an accomplice in the destruction of a friendship. In contrast, if you tried to listen and resolve differences, you sent positive messages and refused to accept a destructive method of dealing with the disagreement.

Keep It Positive

To be successful at resolving differences, you want to avoid turning a disagreement into a major war. Doing so is not easy, but if you keep the elements of inviting friendship in mind, you will start on the right track.

Some of the elements of the invitational approach to friendship may help you resolve differences with your friends and other people in your life. Here are some *inviting* suggestions to remember when resolving conflicts and disagreements with your friends:

- *Identify your position, and state it clearly.* Remember, wanting to is an important part of the inviting process, so you have to express *what you want* clearly to your friends.
- *Listen to others' viewpoints and respond in positive ways.* As you have learned, people have different perceptions of similar events, and it is important that we accept the views of others. This does not mean that we always *agree* with their viewpoints, but we do *accept* them.
- *Be optimistic.* Keep a positive attitude that the problem can be resolved without a fight.
- *Treat others with respect.* When you have a disagreement, avoid name calling and belittling others. Such behavior only adds to the conflict and does nothing to settle disagreements. Consider the feelings of others and use positive messages to express your point of view.
- *Persevere.* Sometimes conflicts can be discouraging and you may want to give up. If the friendship is important to you, and if the current problem is important, be confident that you will help your friend(s) resolve it.

- *Be flexible.* While you want to know your own position and persevere in your friendship, it is also important to remain flexible. This means not being stubborn and unwilling to change some of your ideas.
- *Search for options and alternatives.* When you have a disagreement with a friend, explore all the possibilities that might resolve the issue to the satisfaction of everyone involved. Ask yourself: What am I willing to do to make this friendship work?

Role Play 7-A
Play Ball!

Instructions: Your group leader will choose three students to take the roles of friends getting ready to play baseball with other children, assign them roles of friends 1, 2, and 3, and ask them to read their scripts quietly to become familiar with their roles. Then, the three students will play the scene. After they are finished, the class will discuss what they saw and which friend seemed to be using an *inviting* approach to resolve the disagreement.

Friend 1: What positions do we want to play?

Friend 2: I want to pitch.

Friend 3: No, you always pitch. It's my turn. I never get to pitch.

2: Yes you do. You pitched last time and you were awful. We lost 'cause they scored so many runs!

3: That's a lie—you're a liar. I pitched well, but you can't catch! You made a hundred errors and that's how they scored all their runs. Give me the ball!

1: Wait a minute. I would like to pitch, too, but we can't all do it at the same time! We all want the same thing. What should we do so we can start playing ball?

2: Let me pitch; I'm better than both of you.

3: So what? We should each have a chance to pitch.

1: The other team is waiting for us. We can solve this. Maybe we could rotate? One of us could pitch a couple of innings, and after that the other two could pitch some innings.

3: OK. I'll pitch first.

2: No way. You'll pitch your two innings and then quit on us. I'll go first, and you, quitter, can go last.

3: I'm not a quitter; you're an idiot. If you pitch first, I'm not going to play.

2: Just as I said—a quitter! Go ahead and quit—we don't need you.

1: But I came here to play baseball, and I want both of you on my team to play. We have plenty of time for each of us to pitch. Can we toss a coin to choose who will pitch first?

Listening

Listening is probably the most important behavior you can demonstrate when faced with a conflict with a friend or anyone else. This sounds easy because we all think we listen well. In the heat of an argument, however, our listening skills are most tested. In Activity 7.3, review the *obstacles to listening* and rate your strengths and weaknesses in these five areas.

Role Play 7-B
Listen!

Instructions: Your group leader will choose two students to take the roles of friends having an argument, assign them roles of friends 1 and 2, and ask them to read their scripts quietly to become familiar with their roles. Then, the two students will play the scene. After they are finished, the class will discuss what they saw. Was anyone listening?

Friend 1: I don't like the way you always ignore me when we are with other kids.

Friend 2: You're crazy. I don't ignore you. I'm just trying to have a good time.

Friend 1: But you do ignore me. Every time we get together with other kids, you never listen to my ideas or ask me what I want to do.

Friend 2: *(looking away or doing something)* OK. So what do you want to do today?

1: This is important to me. If you are really my friend, you would care about what I think.

A Smile Is a Curve That Straightens Out Differences
Cartoon 7-A

Name ______________________________ Date ________________

ACTIVITY 7.3
Obstacles to Listening

Instructions: Read each obstacle below, and rate yourself on the scale in the right hand column. Rate yourself by checking either the "Problem" column or "Not a Problem" column. Discuss in class or a small group the behaviors that are most likely to give you a problem when you are listening to a friend, particularly during a disagreement.

	Your Rating	
	Problem	Not a Problem
1. *Talking.* It is impossible to listen to another person's point of view when you are talking at the same time. Do you often talk when someone is trying to explain something to you?	________	________
2. *Getting ready to talk.* Even though you might not talk when someone else is telling you something, you might be *thinking* about what you want to say. If you are thinking about what to say, you cannot listen to what the other person is saying to you.	________	________
3. *Arguing silently.* Sometimes when people disagree with us, we argue with them silently in our minds. It is impossible to listen to others when you are disagreeing with them in your head!	________	________
4. *Being impatient.* Walking away when someone is talking with you because you are in a hurry prevents you from listening fully to him or her. Do you take time to listen completely to what people tell you or do you act impatiently?	________	________
5. *Dividing your attention.* One of the most important traits of a good listener is paying full attention to the person speaking. When people talk to you, do you give them full attention or do you become distracted?	________	________

2: We're wasting time. You said I never ask you what you want to do, so I just asked you. So, what is it?

1: There you go again; ignoring my feelings. I want to know if you want to be friends.

2: This is stupid. Of course we're friends, but you're always complaining about something. Why don't we just decide what to do today? C'mon. I don't have all day. It will be time to go home soon.

1: How will I know that you will listen to me when we are with others?

2: How about playing a video game? We could do that!

1: Not until you listen to me.

2: That's a waste of time. I'll listen to you, OK? Now let's do something.

Role Play 7-C
What Happened?

Instructions: Your leader will choose five students and ask them to leave the classroom and wait outside the door. Each of the five students will be assigned a number 1-5 before they leave the classroom. After the five students leave, the leader will tell the class about this event:

> This weekend I went to the shopping center to buy a present for my friend. When I was leaving the store, I saw that a police officer had stopped Mrs. Thomas, the town mayor, who was standing on the sidewalk. The officer was pointing a finger at Mrs. Thomas, who was frowning and holding a package. Other people were standing and watching. I wondered what was happening.

After the leader reads this event to the class, you will all observe what happens as each classmate is invited back to repeat the story.

Student 1 will come back to the classroom and the leader will tell that student about the event. Student 1 must repeat the story *exactly as he or she heard it* to the next student who comes back to the classroom. Students 2, 3, 4, and 5 will then come back, one at a time, and each one will repeat the story to the next until student 5 has returned and heard about the event.

When student 5 has heard it, the leader will ask him or her to repeat it to the class.

After the role play, the class will decide whether the story changed. What, if anything, was deleted from or added to the story? What part did listening and judging play in these changes to the story?

Breaking Up

There may be times when you try every possible way to resolve problems in a positive manner, but your friends insist on fighting. This is when you have to evaluate the benefit of continuing such relationships. You may decide that it is best not to accept a friend's company any longer.

Occasionally, there are times when you decide not to continue a relationship. We call this *breaking up,* and as an old song says, "breaking up is hard to do." Nevertheless, a relationship that is no longer helpful to you, or one that is harmful to you, is really no longer a friendship. It is an abuse of your faith and trust. Such abuse must be rejected, and the friendship no longer accepted. This brings us to a final question about the inviting process: Whom should you invite?

Whom to Invite

In Section 6, you learned that the process of inviting involves specific steps of inviting yourself and others. Now you have learned that *when to invite* includes the four choices of sending, not sending, accepting, and not accepting invitations. In concluding this section, we now consider *whom* to invite. You might think that positive messages are good for everyone, so you should send them to everyone. You may be right, but it is good to consider with whom to begin your invitations.

Yourself

To become a close friend with others, you must first become friends with yourself. This may seem obvious, but for many people it is very difficult. It may surprise you that some people do not like themselves. People who do not feel good about themselves cannot have the courage, trust, optimism, self-respect, responsibility, and intentionality to develop caring relationships

Gold Nugget

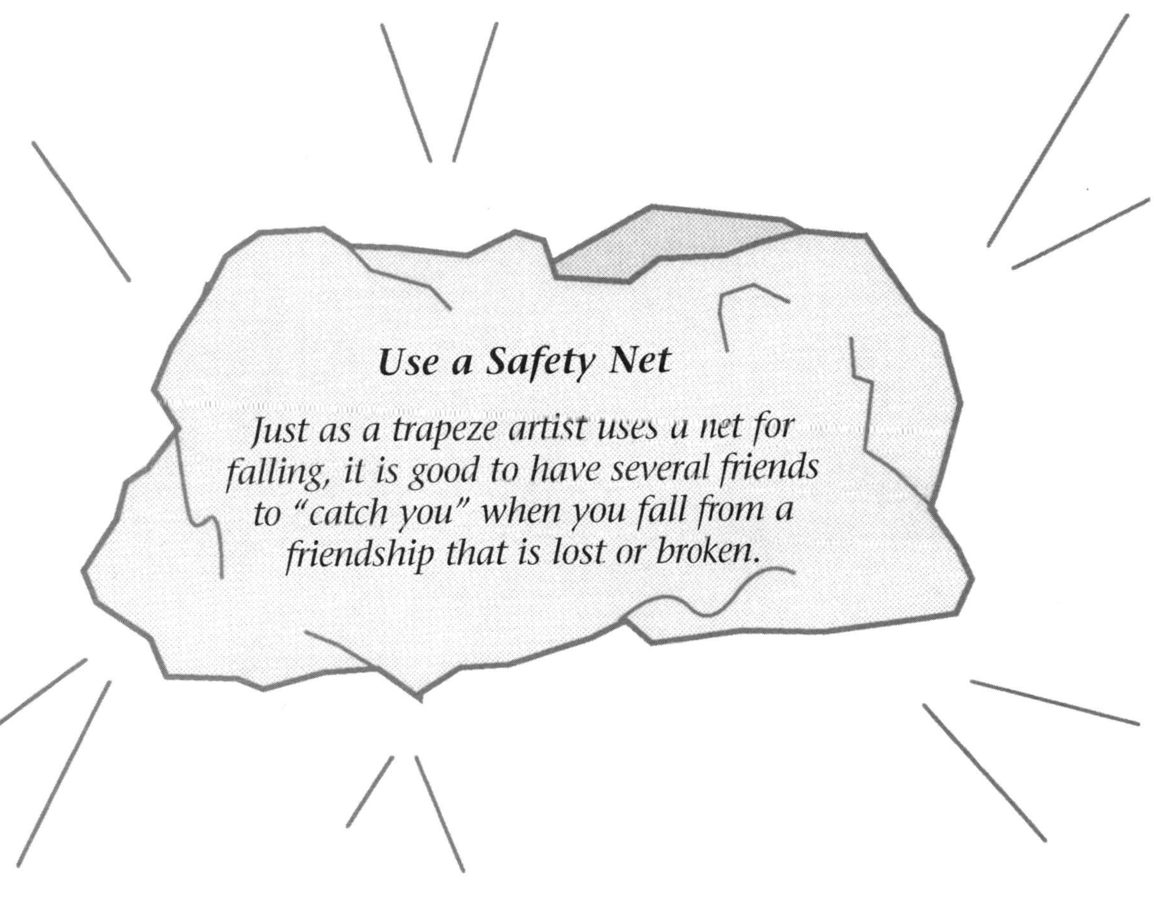

Clearly, invitations start at home. Activity 7.4 will help you recognize invitations.

Family

A second group to whom you can send friendly messages is your family. Include in your family all your immediate relatives—parents, sisters, brothers, grandparents—as well as relatives in your extended family—cousins, aunts, uncles, and others. (Oh yes, don't forget the family pets!) You need support in your life and one of the main sources of support comes from those who love you. Learning to invite these loving relationships is a first step to learning how to invite friendships.

Name ______________________________ Date ______________

ACTIVITY 7.4

Count Your Invitations

During the day write down all the nice things people say to you and do with you. These are all invitations. The next day take this sheet and write down all the invitations you send to others.

Other People's Invitations:

____

____

____

____

____

____

____

____

____

____

My Invitations:

____

____

____

____

____

____

____

____

____

____

Try this activity several times over a period of weeks. The goal is to see if, by increasing the number of positive messages you send to other people, you receive an increasing number of invitations from them. Add more paper to this sheet as you need it.

Myself
Cartoon 7-B

Friends

Returning to an illustration used earlier in this program, you have learned that developing friendships is like cultivating flower gardens. You have to provide the right ingredients so that your garden produces beautiful flowers. Just as flowers need enough water, good soil, sufficient fertilizer, and appropriate sunshine, friendships need a variety of invitations. By consistently inviting your friends in different ways, you will be able to strengthen relationships with them. Friendships that are not nurtured and cared for will, like flower gardens, wither and die away.

Other People

Invitations are important for lasting friendships. They are also important in day-to-day relationships with others. You may not want to form deep relationships with everyone you meet, but by being consistently inviting toward people, you contribute to the community and to the betterment of your fellow students, neighbors, and society. By sending positive messages, you also will discover that new and unexpected friendships develop. Someone once said, "Your dearest friend in all the world was once a total stranger." Use Activities 7.5 and 7.6 for new ways to invite friends.

By inviting family, friends, and others, you will be in a strong position to form and keep many lasting friendships, but to become an inviting friend you should start with yourself. Friends want to associate with people who care about themselves. If you do not treat yourself well, it is unlikely that others will treat you any better. In the next two sections we will explore ways to invite yourself.

Name ______________________________ Date ______________

ACTIVITY 7.5
Want Ad for a Friend

Design an advertisement for a friend that could be placed in a newspaper, in a magazine, or on a billboard. Use pictures and phrases to attract the types of friends you would like to have.

Name ______________________________ Date ________________

ACTIVITY 7.6
Create a "Nugget"

Think of an idea or saying that is important to friendship and write it in the gold nugget. Be sure to give it a name. Share your nugget in class and collect other "nuggets" from your classmates. These ideas will add to your knowledge about making friends.

Gold Nugget

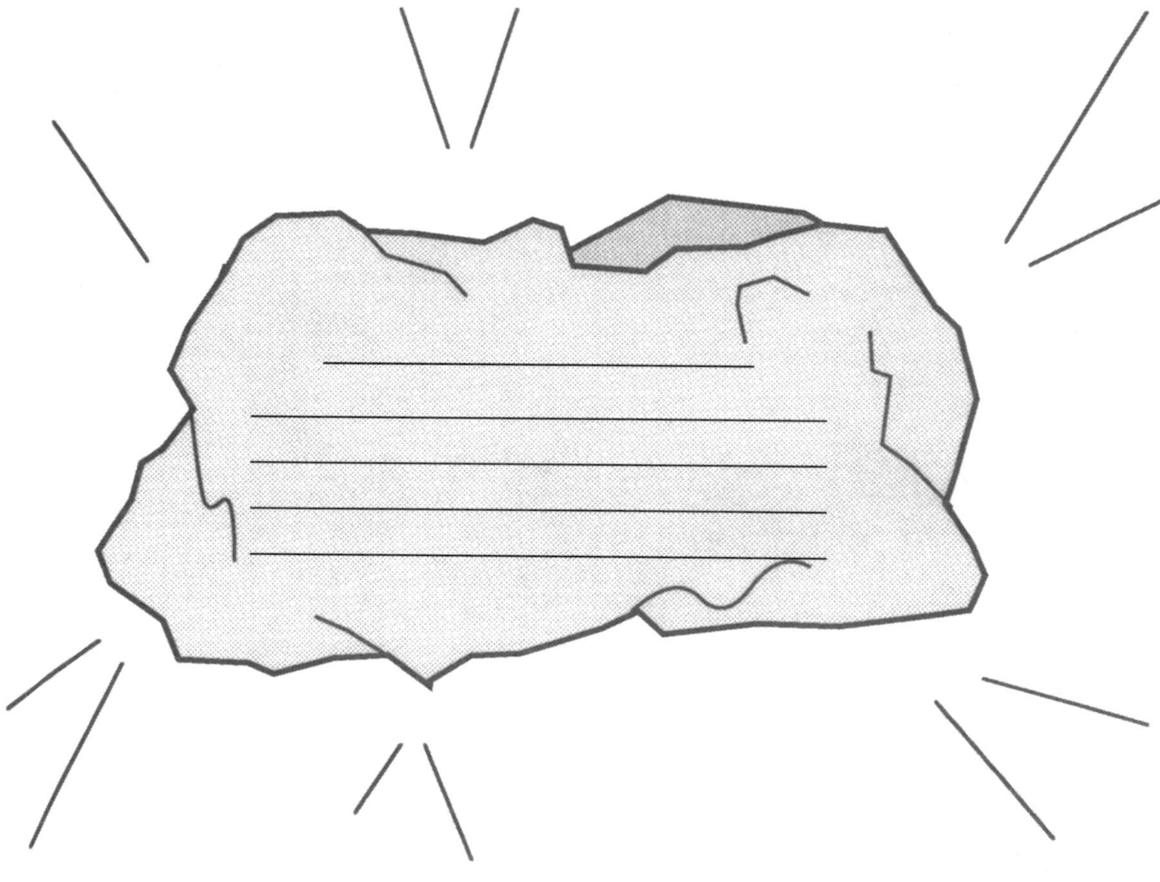

Section 8

CHOOSING POSITIVE BEHAVIORS

GROUP LEADER INSTRUCTIONS

Summary:

This section emphasizes the importance of positive behaviors in building successful friendships. It begins with "Behaving Appropriately" and teaches students self-responsibility in choosing their behaviors. "Doing Unto Others" and "Avoiding Blame" are two themes used to convey the importance of self-responsibility. In addition, the lesson discusses how positive "self-talk" affects the outcome of friendships because it enables students to establish an optimistic stance for themselves.

This section includes two other areas of positive behaviors that influence the friendships students will make in their lives—"Becoming Educated" and "Enjoying Life." In both of these areas, students are encouraged to consider the goals they set, the choices they make, and ultimately, the intention with which they live their lives.

Objectives:

1. To learn about self-responsibility in building friendships.
2. To understand how education affects many other aspects of one's life, including friendships.
3. To explore ways to enjoy life to its fullest.

Activities

Activity 8.1 asks students to evaluate their own behaviors. It lists common behaviors that may be troublesome and asks students to check those that get them into trouble. Students are asked a series of questions about the behaviors they checked, and in particular are asked to consider what would be different if they stopped choosing some of these behaviors. This activity has students self-reflect. It encourages them to look at behaviors *they* believe are problematic and explore what to do about them.

Materials

- ❒ Copies of Activity 8.1
- ❒ Pens and pencils
- ❒ Chart paper or chalkboard to record additional behaviors identified by students

Activity 8.2 has students analyze the story of Bart and Reggie, a friendship that ends. Students are asked to suggest ways that Reggie might have helped his friend Bart so their friendship might have continued. Students can explore the responsibility both partners have in keeping friendships healthy and alive.

Materials

- ❒ Copies of Activity 8.2
- ❒ Pencils or pens
- ❒ Chart paper or chalkboard for large group discussion

Activity 8.3 asks students to write down some of their educational goals. Then they write down specific behaviors they could choose to reach their goals. An example is given. When people write down their goals, it reinforces the commitment they make to themselves. Encourage students to keep these written goals in a visible place at home or school, for example, on their bedroom door or locker door at school.

Materials

- ❒ Copies of Activity 8.3
- ❒ Pencils or pens
- ❒ Chart paper or chalkboard for class to share their goals

Activity 8.4 has students monitor their self-talk and negative behaviors for a week. In particular, two behaviors are monitored: (1) how often students say "I can't," and (2) how often they blame other people when things go wrong. Self-monitoring their behavior can help students see themselves the way their friends and others see them.

MATERIALS

- ❐ Copies of Activity 8.4
- ❐ (Students may also want to use note pads that they can keep in a pocket for this activity.)
- ❐ Pens or pencils

ROLE PLAY

Role Play 8-A asks two students to act out a conversation about creating a Home Page. If your students are unfamiliar with web sites and Home Pages on the Internet, you may want to give a brief lesson. The class observes the role play and evaluates how positive the interaction was. Ask students to look for particular words or phrases that helped them arrive at their evaluation.

VOCABULARY WORDS

These words may need additional explanation by the group leader depending on the reading level of students in the class. Words with an asterisk denote concepts that may need explanation.

civility*
consequences
self-instructing*
adventuresome
critical*
fruitless
routine
mutually*
meditating
specifically
continuous
accomplishment
exchange
enable
impact
demonstrate
gazing
Velcro

CHOOSING POSITIVE BEHAVIORS

Civility costs nothing and buys everything.

Lady Mary Wortley Montagu

As you learned earlier in this program, your behavioral self is an important part of the self-concept that affects friendships. In this section you will examine behaviors and their importance to friendship more closely. In particular, you will learn about choosing behaviors with which to form beneficial and long-lasting friendships.

BEHAVING APPROPRIATELY

Most friendships are established when you create specifically planned positive messages and send those messages to others, and when they in turn accept them. These messages are sent and accepted in the form of the behaviors that you choose to use. This is also true for the messages that you send to yourself.

Section 5 presented a list of behaviors that you read and checked to determine which behaviors you had used during the day. These behaviors were a sample of all the behaviors that help to make up a person's behavioral self. The list was long, and you probably added some of your own behaviors to it. There are many behaviors to choose each day of your life. This is true for the behaviors that you choose when inviting others, and it is also true for the behaviors that you choose to invite yourself.

What is most important is that *you* choose *your* behaviors. You choose what you are going to do, and how you are going to behave. Sometimes people influence you by sending inviting or disinviting messages, but the final decision of how you behave is always up to you. For example, if friends ask you to go to the store with them and your mother is expecting you home, you have the responsibility of deciding which behavior—going to the store or going home—to choose. Once you make that choice, you also have the responsibility for the consequences of the behavior you choose. You can use Activity 8.1 to evaluate your behaviors.

Name ______________________________ Date ______________

ACTIVITY 8.1
Evaluating Behaviors

Check the list of behaviors below and mark the ones that sometimes get you into trouble.

arguing	eating	sulking
sleeping	working	worrying
pretending	daydreaming	gossiping
fighting	laughing	stealing
studying	avoiding	hating
talking	lying	playing
complaining	cheating	cursing

After checking the behaviors, write down any other behaviors that get you in trouble with your friends but are not on the list above.

Now that you have a list of "troubling" behaviors, answer the questions below for each of the behaviors on your list.

1. Is the behavior itself troublesome, or is it the way you use the behavior? ___________

____

____

____

2. Does using the behavior help you in any way? ___________________

____

____

____

3. What would happen if you decided to stop using this behavior? ___________

____

____

____

4. If you wanted to, how could you change this behavior to make it a more positive one? _

____

____

____

Consequences are what happens after you behave a certain way. In the example above, if you decide to go with your friends, one consequence might be that your mother would worry because she would not know where you were. You would be responsible for creating that worrisome situation.

Behaving appropriately and accepting responsibility for behaviors you choose are important ways of inviting yourself. Let us look at a few ideas that can guide you in choosing appropriate behaviors.

Doing Unto Others

The Golden Rule says, "Do unto others as you would have them do unto you." This means that you should always treat other people the way you would like to be treated yourself. If you want to have friends and to be invited by others, then you will want to choose friendly behaviors that invite other people. Treating people in friendly, positive ways helps you establish a posture that says, "I'm a good person." Such a statement tells people that you have the optimistic, trustful, and respectful qualities that they look for in a friend.

The last few words of the Golden Rule are the most important: "... as you would have them do unto you." Notice that it does not say "as they have done unto you." You should treat people the way you want to be treated, not the way you are treated by others.

On occasion, people are mean and nasty; they send disinvitations. When this happens to you, are you mean and nasty in return? If so, you may want to practice the Golden Rule. Sending negative messages in return for disinvitations is not the way to establish friendships. It is only a way to start a war. It does not matter who strikes the first blow. What does matter is who is willing to stop it, and to start behaving more appropriately.

This brings us to another way to check your behaviors. By behaving appropriately and being responsible, you pay attention to your own behaviors and not to what others are doing. You take responsibility for your behaviors and do not blame others for your mistakes.

Avoiding Blame

Too often, friendships end because friends blame each other when things go wrong. It is easy to search for someone else to blame. On the other hand, it is more difficult to stand up and apologize for your mistakes. A true friendship, as you have learned, has such qualities as trust and respect that prevent it from decaying into an atmosphere of blame, distrust, and disrespect. Having the courage to take responsibility and admit your mistakes is a hallmark of true friendship.

There is one caution about avoiding blame. Being responsible for your behavior does not mean you should accept the blame for another's mistakes. A good friendship is based on mutual trust. Each friend, therefore, avoids blaming the other. If you are in a relationship where you accept most of the responsibility when things go

Gold Nugget

wrong, perhaps you need to examine the balance of trust and respect in that friendship. Take responsibility for your own behaviors and expect your friends to take equal responsibility for theirs.

Examining your behaviors and relationships is a continuous process. It is through this examination that you tell yourself what you think about yourself and your relationships with others. Telling yourself, or "self-instructing," is a way of evaluating your behaviors.

Self-Instructing

If you are like most people, there are times when you probably talk to yourself. You may not talk out loud (although some people do), but you say things privately to yourself about your behaviors. Sometimes this self-talk is positive and encouraging. For example, when trying to do a difficult math problem, you might tell yourself, "I know how to do this. I can get the right answer." In this way, you encourage yourself. When you get the answer and solve the problem correctly, you say, "I knew I could!" You tell yourself good things as a reward for your accomplishment.

At other times you might talk to yourself in negative ways. You might worry about what others think, and you say, "Oh, I can't do that. It won't be good. It will look awful." Negative self-instructions prevent you from having the courage to choose appropriate behaviors. People who constantly put themselves down with negative self-talk usually have difficulty making close friends. This is because their negative attitudes about themselves make them difficult to be around. An example of how self-talk can affect a friendship is seen in the story of Bart and Reggie.

BART AND REGGIE

Bart and Reggie were friends. They were together often, they were in the same class at school, and they belonged to the same Boy Scout troop. Reggie liked to try new things. He was adventuresome. Bart, on the other hand, worried about trying new things. He often thought, "I won't be able to do this as well as Reggie." Because Bart spent so much time in negative self-talk, he frequently shied away from doing things with Reggie. For example, when the scouts built a new ropes course with a swinging bridge, a rope ladder, and a Tarzan vine, Bart would not take his turn on the course. Of course, his friend Reggie was one of the first boys to try it.

As time went by and new adventures and activities were planned, Reggie made new friends in scouts and at school. Not all of these activities were risky like the ropes course, yet Bart continued to tell himself, "I can't do that." Because he was unwilling to try new things, Bart did not make many new friends, and he became somewhat of a loner. As Reggie made new friends, his friendship with Bart became less important, and eventually their friendship ended.

Use Activity 8.2 to think about how Reggie might have helped their friendship.

Self-instructing can be either positive or negative. Everyone self-talks, so it is important to learn positive self-instructions that will help you choose appropriate behaviors. You want to choose behaviors that will foster helpful friendships. One way to improve your self-instruction is by keeping a sharp mind. This means learning more and taking pride in your education. Education is another important area for inviting yourself.

Name ______________________ Date ____________

ACTIVITY 8.2
Reggie's Turn

If you were Reggie in the story of Bart and Reggie, what would you have done to help keep your friendship with Bart alive? Write down some suggestions for Reggie and share these in class. Do you think Reggie has a responsibility to help Bart with his negative self-talk?

Suggestions for Reggie: ______________________

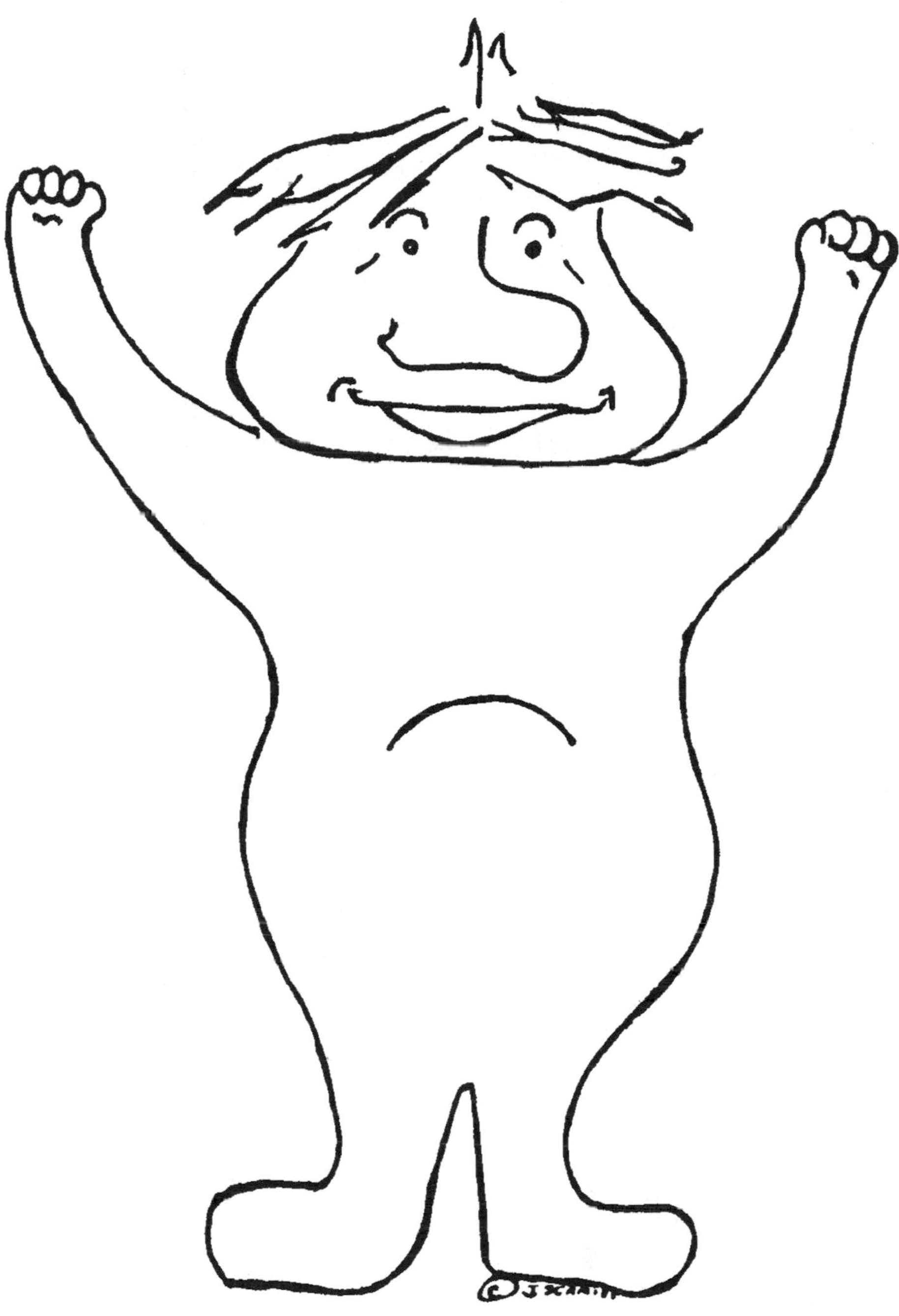

I Know I Can
Cartoon 8-A

Gold Nugget

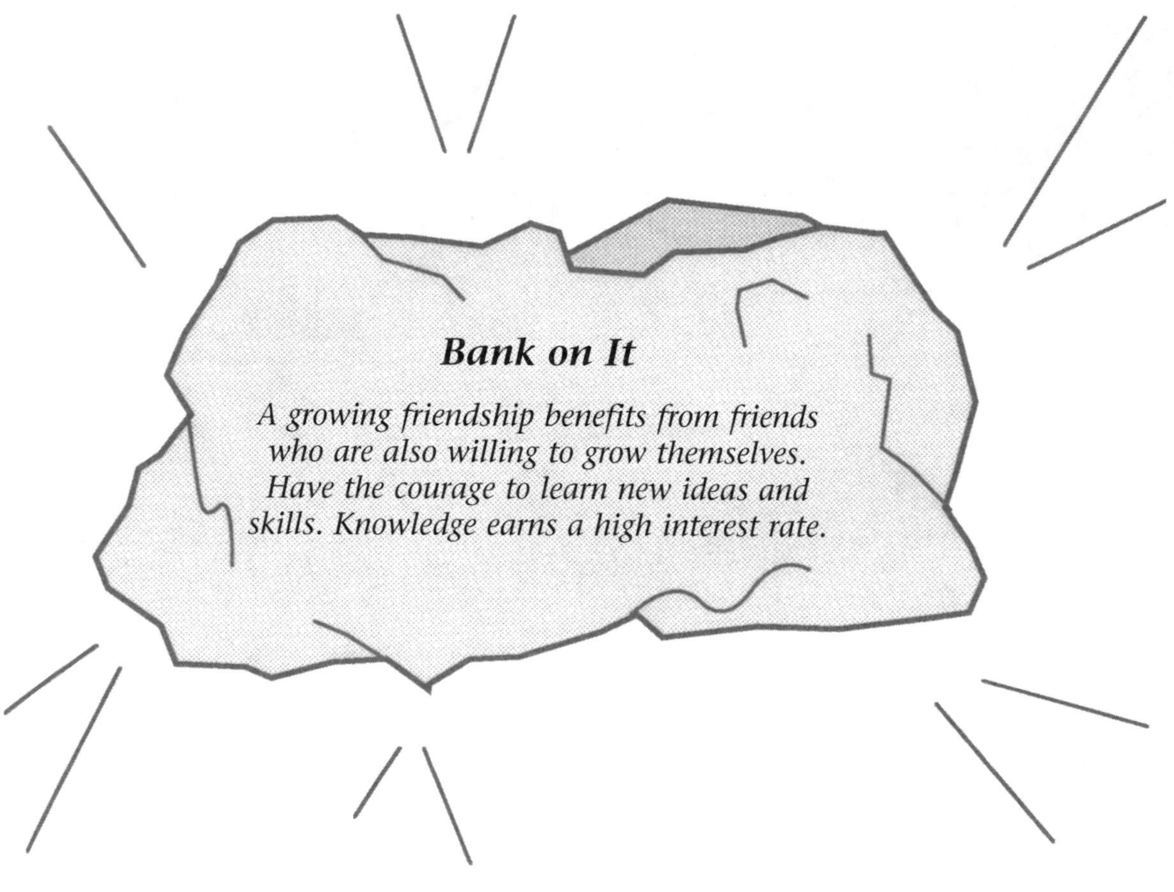

Becoming Educated

People form friendships because they want to share with others, want to help others, want to be a part of others' lives, and want to get as much out of life as possible. Sharing your life means having something to share. One of the most important things you can share with others is your knowledge.

Friendships thrive on the exchange of ideas, information, and wisdom. Earlier in this program you read how close friends can help when you have difficult decisions to make. This is one of the reasons people want friends, so they can rely on friendly advice during difficult times. Because your friends will want to rely on you, it is important that you have reliable information to share with them. This means becoming educated.

Learning and gaining knowledge are critical areas of human development. They are also necessary conditions for friendship. Most people search for friends who want to experience life, want to grow, and want to achieve in areas that enable them to be successful. Becoming educated is directly related to your ability to achieve and enjoy life. Whether you want to achieve in art, sports, business, or other areas, education will play a vital role in your success—and that success will contribute to the friendships you form.

As with friendship, education does not happen by accident. It takes intention and planning. In school, your teachers, principals, and counselors help with your education, but if you do not intend to learn, all their help might be fruitless. At home, your parents, grandparents, and others guide your education, but if you do not listen to their guidance, you will not learn. In the next three sections, you will learn about education and its impact on friendship. First, you will learn about planning educational goals.

Having Goals

To begin inviting yourself educationally, you must first decide what areas of education are important to you. In school, many areas of education are decided for you. Reading, writing, math, science, and social studies are a few subjects that give you a basic education. These subjects are chosen for you by the school. Beyond what you learn in school, however, it is good to choose additional areas of education that are important to you. For example, you might be interested in sports, music, or art, or perhaps you have a deep interest in one of the school subjects, such as science. If you know of these interests, you can plan ways to become more educated in these areas. Use Activity 8.3 to begin your educational plan.

Planning to become more educated means setting goals for yourself. For example, suppose that you were very interested in swimming. You were not only interested in learning the basics of swimming, but also in becoming a great swimmer who would compete in major national and international swimming events. If you had such an interest, you would begin setting goals to become a great swimmer. You would join a swim team in your town. You would practice regularly. You would plan an exercise routine with your coach to develop muscles for swimming. And, you would probably make friends with other boys and girls who had a similar interest in swimming. All of these activities would help you achieve your goal to become a successful swimmer.

Inviting yourself to become educated will influence the friends you make throughout your lifetime. It will influence your friendships during your school-age years, and it will influence your friendships in adulthood. By caring about your education, you also demonstrate another way that you care about yourself. Caring for yourself educationally does not end when you finish school. Rather, it is a lifelong process of learning.

Name ______________________ Date ____________

ACTIVITY 8.3
My Educational Plan

Write down three educational goals you have. Next to each goal, write one behavior you could choose to help you reach that goal. This is a beginning plan for you to reach each of your goals. You can use the extra space to write down hopes and dreams that may later become goals.

Educational Goals	*Behaviors to Reach My Goals*
(Example) Improve in math	Spend 15 minutes a day practicing math problems

Learning for Life

Even though much of your learning is taking place in school right now, you also learn quite a bit on your own outside school. Learning in school is important, and you can invite yourself in this learning process by forming good study habits, behaving appropriately in class, and doing assignments on time. Learning on your own, however, is equally important, and can be developed by the books, magazines, and newspapers you read, the athletic teams you play on, the clubs and religious groups you join, and the hobbies you take up. When inviting yourself to become more educated, it is essential to realize that learning goes on forever.

This idea of lifelong learning can be applied to friendships as well. You have read that friendships, like gardens, require attention and caring. Friendships that are neglected become wilted and unproductive. Part of caring for your friendships means being willing to learn and do new things. Friendships that constantly repeat events, fail to search for opportunities, and refuse to accept new experiences tend to die from boredom. Friendships, as with life in general, are successful when they seek mutually beneficial learning experiences. These experiences should enlighten, entertain, and educate. While at times education can be hard work, in friendship it can also be fun.

Role Play 8-A
The Home Page

Instructions: Your group leader will choose two students to take the roles of friends who decide to create a computer Home Page about their friendship. The leader will assign them roles of friends 1 and 2 and ask them to read their scripts quietly to become familiar with their roles. Then the two students will play the scene. After they are finished, the class will discuss what they saw and evaluate how positive or negative the interaction was. What words helped the class evaluate the relationship?

Friend 1: I've got a great idea. My dad has subscribed to the Internet and we could set up a Home Page about ourselves.

Friend 2: Neat. My archeology club set up a Home Page about our club, and we hear from kids from all over the world. If we set up a page about ourselves we might hear from other kids in other states or even far away countries.

Friend 1: Yeah. How should we start? We need a name for our page.

Friend 2: How about the Friendship Club? That way we will hear from other kids who are interested in friendship.

Summa Cum Friendship
Cartoon 8-B

1: Great! I like the way you think! But what if there is already a Friendship Club on the Web? Maybe we need to give our club a special name.

2: How about our first initials? The ______ & ______ Friendship Club.

1: I like that! Now, we need to decide what to put on our Home Page.

2: Hum-m-m. Gosh, there's so much. I don't know where to start.

1: What if we just start making a list of what we want on the Home Page? Then we can narrow down the list and plan a format later.

2: OK. I'll write things down as we make our list. Let's begin.

Learning for Fun

Sharing a learning experience with friends can be fun and rewarding. Learning does not have to be a drag. Too often when a task seems difficult, people assume a negative attitude and self-talk their way into misery. Maybe you have heard students talking this way in school: "This is too hard. It's stupid; why do we have to learn this? We will never use this stuff." Learning is sometimes hard, but that does not mean it cannot be enjoyable.

Use your friendships in ways that help you to enjoy learning. For example, if you are studying for a spelling test and you do not like spelling, ask a friend to study with you by making up a spelling contest. Turn your studying into fun by pretending you are on a television game show and the winner gets to take a rocket trip to the moon! The point is that friendships can help you to work hard and play hard at the same time.

Not all of life is fun. Sometimes bad things happen and sometimes learning is not very easy. By using your friendships, you can minimize the hard times. Frequently, things are not as bad as you tell yourself. Friendships help you see the good things you can get out of tough situations. Finding benefits in difficult situations is one way of enjoying life.

ENJOYING LIFE

The first two parts of this section—Behaving Appropriately, and Becoming Educated—have one common goal. They each contribute to an enjoyable life. People who enjoy their lives want to share that joy with others, and they want to help other people enjoy their lives as well; that is the reason for friendship. In this section, you have learned that by behaving appropriately and becoming educated you will improve your chances of forming and keeping close, beneficial friendships. The establishment of these friendships will help you enjoy your life more fully.

Inviting yourself to enjoy life is the first step to forming enjoyable friendships. Again, as with behaving and becoming educated, the choice is yours. The extent to which you enjoy your life will depend on how much you *intend* to enjoy it. Learn to avoid the word *can't* (Activity 8.4). Sadly, there are people who go through life saying, "There is no party." As a result, they do not enjoy themselves. What they fail to realize is that one sure way to enjoy life is to have the party yourself! And invite all your friends! You will enjoy life if you invite yourself to your own celebration.

Gold Nugget

Name ______________________________ Date ______________

ACTIVITY 8.4
Catch Yourself

Every time you catch yourself using the word "can't," write it down—or if you find yourself blaming others when things do not go the way that you would like them to, make note of it. You will know you are blaming others if you use phrases like "You should have," or "It's your fault!" See how many times you use the word "can't" or blame others during a week. If you use the word "can't" often, you might be missing opportunities for learning, adventure, or enjoyment in your relationships. If you find that you frequently blame others when things go wrong, you might be jeopardizing the trust that your friends have in you.

Celebrating Life

There are limitless ways to celebrate life. For example, going shopping, having a slumber party, getting a group together for a football game or a movie, helping plan a school dance, volunteering to clean up the church grounds, and many other activities demonstrate ways of celebrating friendship and life.

Celebrating life does not always have to be a big blast. There are many simple ways to enjoy yourself. Cuddling up with a favorite book, listening to music with your best friend, relaxing with a pet, sending a "Miss you" card to a friend who has moved away, and going out to see the stars at night are a few simple ways that you can celebrate life. Sometimes it is the simple things in life that you overlook. Gazing at the stars is a good example. Someone once said that if the stars were visible only once a year, everyone would go out to see them. Because the stars are always there, we take their beauty for granted.

Celebrating life means not taking things for granted. It means having the big party as well as enjoying simple pleasures. A trip to a theme park, a day at the zoo, an hour alone watching television, fishing in a quiet stream, or meditating in your place of worship can each in their own way contribute to your celebration of life. What is important is that you plan ways to celebrate with others as well as taking time for yourself.

Taking Time Alone

The human mind and body can only stand so much activity at one time. It is wise on occasion to energize yourself. This process of energizing not only helps you, but also helps your friendships. Friendships, like electronic toys, need energy; they do not run on their own. Energy in friendships comes in the form of positive messages sent to yourself and others.

Sometimes friendships are energized when friends are apart. Friends who are always together take the risk that the freshness and excitement of their friendship may wear thin. For this reason, friends need some time alone to do things for themselves without any guidance or interference from others. During these times alone, you can learn new things to share with your friends when you come together again.

Perhaps in the past, you have had a friend who stuck to you like Velcro. After a while you got tired of this person "hanging on" all the time. Because your "Velcro friend" would not leave you any time for yourself, you ended the friendship.

True friends respect the space of others. They have no need to "hang on," and they recognize the importance of spending time alone or with other friends. Inviting yourself to spend a little quality time alone may be the best way to ensure lasting friendships. It also gives you time to evaluate the friendships you have and to consider new friendships to form.

In this section, you have explored ideas about choosing positive behaviors to establish beneficial friendships, becoming educated, and enjoying life. In the final section, we continue this exploration, but direct our attention toward the most important friend you will ever choose—yourself.

Gold Nugget

Make No-Stick Contracts
Friends can be close without smothering each other. Be sure you give your friends enough space to breathe.

Section 9

SENDING YOURSELF INVITATIONS

GROUP LEADER INSTRUCTIONS

Summary:

This final section encourages students to explore more thoroughly the idea of sending positive messages to themselves. Students are asked to focus on parts of their *selves* that will help them form beneficial friendships. In emphasizing this topic, the section revisits two themes; the first is *knowing yourself* and the second is *having the desire to change*. Both of these themes are reviewed and extended to include additional topics to help students treat themselves well. These additional topics are listed under the heading, "Living Healthy" and include: "Eating and Drinking Well," "Resting and Exercising," "Keeping Clean, " and "Tuning Your Psyche."

Each of these ideas is described briefly and stories, activities, Gold Nuggets, and role plays reinforce the lessons. The program concludes with a brief summary and activities about making friends.

Objectives

1. To focus on ways that students can learn to send positive messages to themselves.
2. To learn how positive self-messages put students in position to build healthy friendships.

Activities

Activity 9.1 first asks students to analyze traits they like about themselves and that other people like about them as well. Second, students are asked to analyze traits they do not like about themselves and identify the traits they cannot change. This activity has students continue their self-reflection. It encourages them to look at traits *they* believe are positive and those that are negative, and determine whether or not they can change any of them.

Materials

- ❐ Copies of Activity 9.1
- ❐ Pens and pencils
- ❐ Chart paper or chalkboard for class discussion of traits identified by students

Activity 9.2 instructs students to record on a weekly chart things they eat and drink. Writing down a weekly record of one's diet can be revealing about healthy or unhealthy eating habits. It is never too early to begin proper nutrition.

Materials

- ❐ Copies of Activity 9.2
- ❐ Pencils or pens

Activity 9.3 tells students about famous people who struggled before they became successful. Louis Armstrong, Winston Churchill, Oprah Winfrey, Dave Thomas, and Wilma Rudolph are mentioned. Students are asked to think of other famous people who either had difficulties or failed before they became famous. Students are also asked to think of a difficulty they have had in their lives and write about what they did to overcome this problem.

Materials

- ❐ Copies of Activity 9.3
- ❐ Pens or pencils

Activity 9.4 is an enjoyable exercise to demonstrate that sometimes things look easy but may be difficult to do. The "Novak Shuffle" is used to teach this idea. Students can discuss what it takes to be successful at something that looks easy, but may be difficult, such as practice, patience, watching, and learning from others.

MATERIALS

- ❐ Instructions for Activity 9.4
- ❐ Copies of the cartoon for the "Novak Shuffle"

Activity 9.5 asks students to draw a nebbish similar to the ones used throughout the book. This is an enjoyable activity that allows students to express friendship ideas in cartoon form.

MATERIALS

- ❐ Copies of Activity 9.5
- ❐ Pencils, crayons, or other art media

Activity 9.6 invites students to treat themselves by planning something nice for themselves and carrying out their plan. This activity incorporates many of the ideas learned in this book. Planning positive messages and acting upon one's plan are foundations for inviting friendship.

MATERIALS

- ❐ Copies of Activity 9.6

ROLE PLAY

Role Play 9-A has individual students pretend they are talking to themselves in a mirror. Students think of something they want to change in their lives, and proceed to talk to the mirror about their plan as if they were explaining it to someone else. As the class members watch these role plays, they should record words and phrases that illustrate the following:

1. Optimistic messages
2. Self-responsibility
3. Courage to change
4. Healthy views of oneself

VOCABULARY WORDS

These words may need additional explanation by the group leader depending on the reading level of students in the class. Words with an asterisk denote concepts that may need explanation.

admiration
acceptance
position*
encyclopedia
reality*
determining
alcohol
imbalance*
sufficient
infection
handicap
frequency

emphasized
characteristics
demonstrates
essential
ingredients
beverages
moderation*
strenuous
irritable
reluctant
maintenance*
duration

SENDING YOURSELF INVITATIONS

It is a delight to discover people who are worthy of admiration and respect and love, but it is vital to believe yourself deserving of these things.

Jo Coudert

You have learned about friendship and about a special way of inviting friendships. A recurring theme emphasized throughout this program is that you will form friendships more easily if you start by inviting yourself. In this section, you will explore more thoroughly this idea of sending yourself positive messages.

As with forming friendships, the process of inviting yourself requires intention on your part. You have learned that the meaning of intention is to have direction and purpose. To invite yourself, you must have a plan to make things happen. This section will help you plan positive messages to send to yourself. These messages will enable you to grow and become a healthy, happy, and successful person—a person with whom other people would want to be friends.

Developing a plan for inviting yourself includes focusing on parts of your self that will help you form friendships with others. In Section 8, you learned about the behavioral and educational parts of the self, and how they can be important in forming friendships. In this section we continue to focus on you and how you can establish a plan for becoming a friend. The first step is to get started.

GETTING STARTED

Every plan has a beginning. A plan to invite yourself starts with you. Getting started means choosing the parts of yourself that you believe are important in forming friendships, and deciding what you can do, or not do, to change or improve those parts of yourself. An important idea to remember about the self, and one that you learned earlier, is that some parts of the self are facts and some are beliefs that you have about yourself.

Gold Nugget

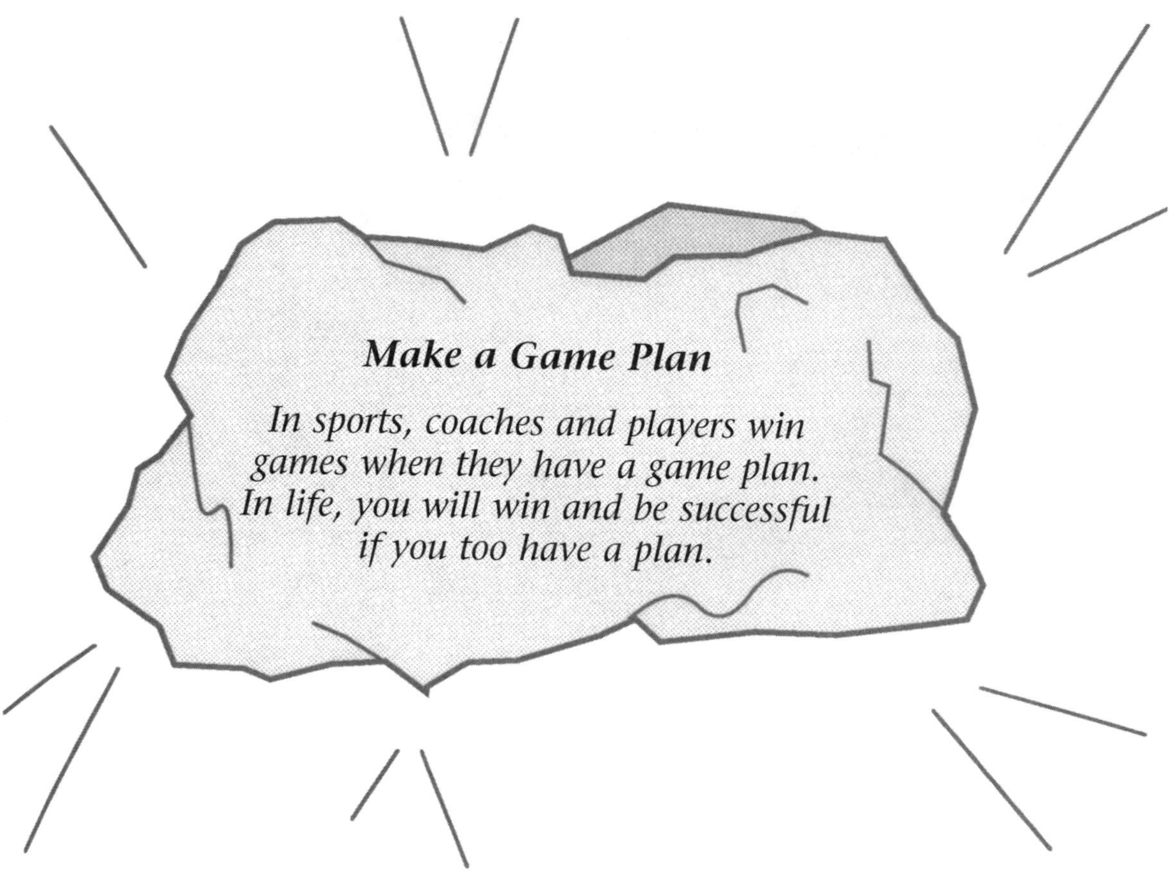

You control your beliefs. This means that you can change what you believe. For example, if you believe that you are too tall and no one would want to be your friend, you could change that belief by saying, "I'm taller than most kids my age, but I can still be friends with many of them."

Facts are not always as easy to control or change as your beliefs. Some facts you can change, but others you cannot. In the example above, it would be impossible to change how tall or short you are. You have to learn to live with those kinds of facts. On occasion, facts can be changed. For example, if you ask someone to a party and that person says "no," you might be able to get an acceptance to your invitation by changing the time, date, or other fact about the party.

In some ways, changing facts may take more work than changing your beliefs; yet, because people believe so strongly in some things, it is often difficult for them to change those beliefs. Sadly, some people hold onto beliefs even when they are hurting themselves or others by doing so. When this happens, it is unlikely that people will make many close and lasting friendships. To make close, lasting friendships, it is important to know the facts about yourself and the beliefs you have about those facts.

Knowing Yourself

Inviting friendships is based largely on your ability to know yourself and to find traits in others that match or balance the characteristics in yourself. Taking time to examine yourself and learn about your strengths and weaknesses helps to determine the areas of your life that must change if you are going to be successful in your friendships.

Getting to know yourself is not always easy. You have only one view of the world, and it is difficult to turn your eyes toward yourself and learn who you truly are. To know yourself better, you must rely on your own self-perceptions as well as the perceptions of others. You can use Activity 9.1 to help you with those perceptions.

Before making a plan to change things about yourself, you might want to check your perceptions with other people. To do that, you can take your two lists from the activity above to friends or family members and ask them these questions: What do you like about me? What do you not like about me? Compare their answers with yours and add their perceptions. Be prepared for some surprises. Often, people's perceptions of us are quite different from those we have of ourselves. The more people you ask, the more complete your lists will be.

When you have established the traits you like and those you do not like, you will be in a position to make changes. This information will help you move to the next step, which is to have the desire to change.

Having the Desire to Change

You will remember that the first step of inviting is *wanting to.* Now that you have begun to *know yourself* through your own eyes and through the eyes of others, it is time to decide what you want to do with this knowledge. What strengths do you have that will help you form friendships, and what weaknesses do you have that you want to change? Making these decisions demonstrates that you *want to* invite yourself.

Many people go through life knowing that they want to change, yet they never permit themselves to act on that knowledge. Having the desire to change may be as important as, or more important than, the knowledge of what you want to be different. Knowledge is the first step, but desire is what makes change a reality. It is similar to baking a cake. You might know the ingredients needed and you might know

Name ______________________________ Date ________________

ACTIVITY 9.1
Seeing Yourself

Your self-perceptions can be examined by making a checklist about yourself. Make a list of the things you like about yourself. When you have finished the list, check the items that you believe others also like about you.

What I Like About Myself	**What Other People Like Too**
______________________________	______________________________
______________________________	______________________________
______________________________	______________________________
______________________________	______________________________

How many items did you check that other people like about you? Are there some items not marked? Do your friends not think these items are good traits? Or do your friends not know that you like these traits about yourself? No matter how you answer these questions, you can do something about it. For example, if you like something about yourself, but your friends do not know it, you can tell them! This is something you can control.

Now make a list of all the things you do not like about yourself. After you have finished the list, check the facts that you cannot change.

What I Do Not Like About Myself	**What I Cannot Change**
______________________________	______________________________
______________________________	______________________________
______________________________	______________________________
______________________________	______________________________
______________________________	______________________________

The items you checked are the things about yourself that you may have to live with. Becoming aware of these facts is important because, if you go through life being miserable about things you cannot change, you will probably not be successful in friendship. The remaining things on your list—the ones you can change—provide a starting point for you to invite yourself.

how to mix those ingredients, but unless you do it and put the pan in the oven, the cake will not be baked!

Knowing yourself and having the desire to change are two important factors when inviting friendships. Doing things that help you know yourself and help you develop the desire to change will get you started toward sending positive messages to yourself and inviting friendship with others. The remainder of this section will focus on areas that are important to your self-development and to lasting friendships—areas related to your physical and mental health.

LIVING HEALTHILY

Much of what you decide to do in your life will be related in some way to how physically able you are and how well you think about yourself and others. Poor health

Gold Nugget

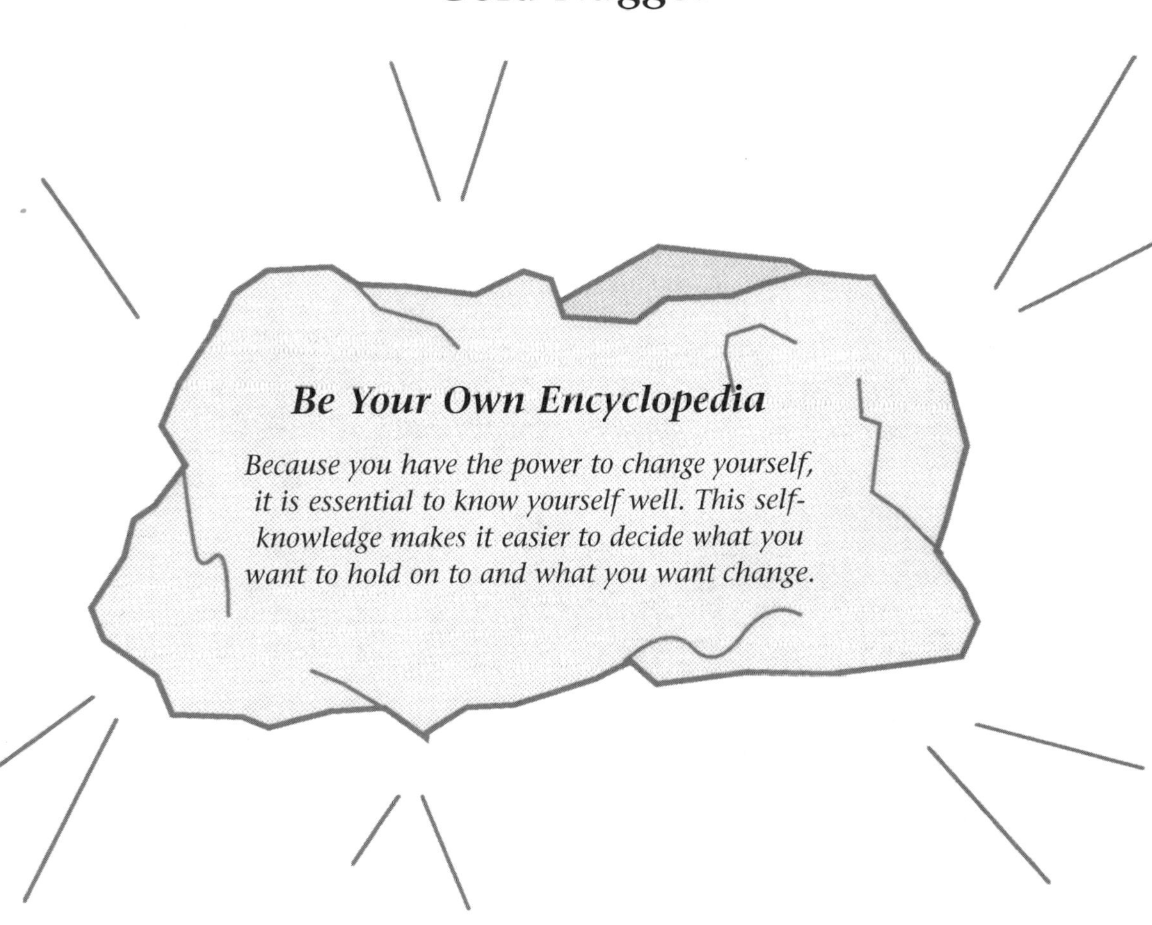

and distorted thinking are two reasons why people choose not to do things for themselves—why they choose not to invite themselves.

Often, people say, "Oh, I would like to do that, but I just don't feel up to it." Not feeling up to it is a frequent excuse for not inviting yourself. On other occasions you might hear people say, "No one wants to be my friend. Everybody hates me, so I hate everybody." This kind of unhealthy thinking is also a reason why some people have difficulty in their friendships.

How well you take care of your body and your mind affects many other aspects of your life, including the energy and effort you put into your friendships. Each of us is given only one body, so it is important that we take the best care of it. To begin, you should put only the best ingredients into your body.

Eating and Drinking Well

Food and drink create the fuel that keeps your body alive. The quality and quantity of food and drink are important factors to consider in determining how well you will live. In terms of quality, there are good foods and beverages and there are not such good foods and beverages. By the same token, there can be too little food and drink, or too much food and drink.

Choose foods and drinks that you know are good for you. Enjoy snacks and sweets on occasion, but avoid making meals of them. Eat balanced meals that satisfy your body's vitamin and mineral requirements. The same can be said for drinks. Sodas and pop are fine for occasional treats, but your body needs a steady diet of dairy products, juices, and water. Drink plenty of water. It is the most natural and beneficial beverage on earth. Use Activity 9.2 to record what you eat and drink.

While on the subject of what to put into your body, it is a good time to mention a warning about such dangerous substances as tobacco, drugs, and alcohol. As you grow older, you will be faced with many decisions, such as "Do I want to smoke cigarettes or do I want to drink alcohol?" These will be critical questions for you and only you can answer them. By establishing healthy eating and drinking habits at an early age, you will be in a stronger position to make appropriate, adult decisions later in life.

Many people have a strong bias against smoking, and it appears that the most recent health studies confirm our beliefs about this dangerous habit—smoking cigarettes is bad. It is bad for the smoker, and it is bad for others who breathe the smoker's smoke. The best decision for you and your body (as well as your family's and friends' bodies) is DON'T SMOKE.

Whatever you decide about eating and drinking, these two rules may be helpful:

1. Almost everything you eat or drink makes a difference to your body. Remember what you learned earlier about invitations? *Everything counts*. Whatever you put into your body—food, drink, or other substances—makes either a positive, nourishing difference or a negative, damaging one.

Name ______________________________ Date ______________

ACTIVITY 9.2
What I Eat and Drink

Use this activity sheet to chart what you eat for a week. During each day of the week, write down everything you eat. Be sure to record snack foods and drinks. This sample week gives you an idea of how healthily you are eating. Check the foods and drinks that are not too healthy for you. Do you think the number of unhealthy foods is too high? If so, this is a behavior you can control.

Monday
Breakfast: ______________________________
Lunch: ______________________________
Dinner: ______________________________
Snack Foods and Beverages: ______________________________

Tuesday
Breakfast: ______________________________
Lunch: ______________________________
Dinner: ______________________________
Snack Foods and Beverages: ______________________________

Wednesday
Breakfast: ______________________________
Lunch: ______________________________
Dinner: ______________________________
Snack Foods and Beverages: ______________________________

Thursday
Breakfast: ______________________________
Lunch: ______________________________
Dinner: ______________________________
Snack Foods and Beverages: ______________________________

Friday
Breakfast: ______________________________
Lunch: ______________________________
Dinner: ______________________________
Snack Foods and Beverages: ______________________________

Saturday
Breakfast: ______________________________
Lunch: ______________________________
Dinner: ______________________________
Snack Foods and Beverages: ______________________________

Sunday
Breakfast: ______________________________
Lunch: ______________________________
Dinner: ______________________________
Snack Foods and Beverages: ______________________________

2. If you decide to eat or drink something that is not nourishing, such as sweets, do so in moderation. Eat or drink a little and then stop. Moderation allows you to enjoy occasional treats. Without moderation early in life, you may find later that you will not be allowed to have any treats at all. Because of weight, heart condition, sugar imbalance, or other problems, your physician will advise you that continued snacking could kill you.

Resting and Exercising

Another area of healthy living is how you use your body. Throughout your life your body will require exercise so that your muscles stay in proper shape. Exercising keeps your body in tune so that damage is avoided when muscles are called upon to do strenuous work. Exercising also makes you fit so that you can keep up the pace with others.

Gold Nugget

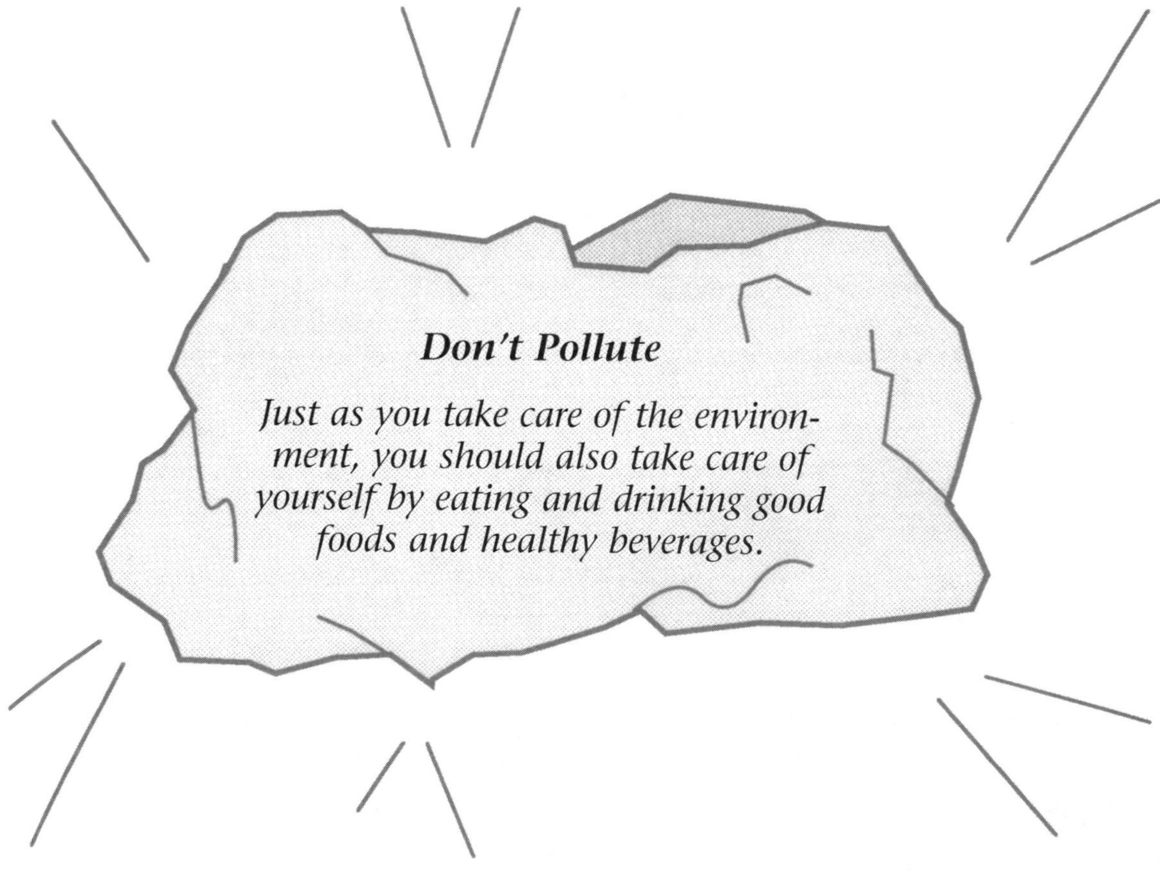

Sometimes your friends may want to do activities that take a lot of energy. Being fit and keeping up with them will help you to invite their continued friendship. The story of Betsy shows how not staying in shape affected her friendships.

"SLOW DOWN" BETSY

Betsy was slightly overweight and she did not get much exercise. Rather than be active, she would sit at home, eat snacks, and watch television all afternoon and evening. Her friends liked having Betsy around because she was nice and had a good sense of humor. But when she was with them, Betsy would often ask her friends to "slow down" or "stop a minute" so that she could catch up or rest. For example, when shopping at the mall, she would always want to sit on a bench for a while. When her friends did not slow down enough, she would whine and complain. Eventually, Betsy's friends stopped inviting her to join them because they got tired of waiting for her to catch up, and they became annoyed with her frequent whining. A little less television watching and a little more exercise might have helped Betsy keep up with her friends.

In addition to exercise, your body needs sufficient rest. Your body is not a machine that can run continuously without a break. Making sure that you go to bed at a reasonable hour and get plenty of rest invites yourself to have enough energy each day to do the tasks expected of you and to do other things that you want to do for yourself. Without sufficient rest, you cannot function well. Not only will you fail to keep up with everyone else, but your tiredness will also affect your mood and attitude.

Have you ever known someone who, when he or she got sleepy, became difficult to get along with? That is what happens to most people when they have not had enough rest. Irritable and difficult people do not make very good friends. By getting plenty of rest and sufficient exercise, your body will be in optimal shape to keep up with the "friendship pace."

Keeping Clean

A third way of being healthy is keeping your body clean. Uncleanliness affects your ability to form friendships in two ways. First, uncleanliness contributes to infection and sickness. If you are always feeling sickly or having problems with infections, it will be hard to keep many close friends. Sometimes illnesses are unavoidable. When they are, your friends will stand by you and try to help. But when your sicknesses or diseases are caused by your continuous lack of health care and inappropriate behavior, friends will lose patience with you. They will be less likely to call on you in the future.

Another way that uncleanliness affects your friendships is by the unpleasant odors from your body and your clothes. Keeping clean sends an invitation to yourself and to those around you. It sends the message that you care about yourself. If you do not care about how clean you are, then others may not care to be near you. You might remember that *proximity* was one factor mentioned in the first section of this program that relates to choosing friends. It means *nearness*. If your body is unclean and has unpleasant odors, it is unlikely that anyone will want to be close to you.

A factor related to cleanliness is good grooming. People who care about their appearance are usually accepted by others. This is logical. If you care about yourself and how clean and neat you look, chances are that you will care about others and they, in turn, will care about you. In contrast, if you do not help yourself look nice, then you probably do not care about yourself and may not care about others. When others read the signal that you do not care about yourself, they will be reluctant to send messages that they want to be your friend.

There are some physical facts about yourself that cannot be changed, but good grooming is something you can control. Good grooming means making the best of what you have. By being clean and looking your best, you send a friendly signal to others.

Tuning Your Psyche

Another area of being healthy is having a strong and stable mind. This means being psychologically and educationally healthy. The Greek word for mind is *psyche* and our English word *psychology* has to do with the study and knowledge of the human mind and behavior. When people are psychologically healthy, they think and behave in positive and helpful ways. On the other hand, when people have psychological problems, their thoughts and behaviors give them trouble.

Sometimes people have trouble in their friendships because they think they are so much better than others, or they think they are not as good as others. Both of these kinds of thinking can handicap a person when making friends. Friends do not want to associate with people who think they are superior, nor do they want to be with people who constantly worry, put themselves down, or complain about how bad their lives are. These kinds of thinking are related to the self-talk explained earlier in this program.

Sometimes we learn about famous people, but we do not always know how these people had to overcome odds to reach their success. In Activity 9.3, you can read about some famous people who, earlier in their lives, had great difficulty or who faced many failures as they were achieving their success. The important lesson in these cases is that they did not let setbacks deter them from their goals.

When you feel that your thinking and behaving are becoming a problem for you—when they prevent you from forming friendships—you may want to seek help from someone. You could start by talking with your parents, a minister, a teacher, or

Name ______________________________ Date ______________

ACTIVITY 9.3
Overcoming the Odds

Read each of the accounts below. In class, discuss other famous people who overcame great odds or repeated failures to be successful. When you have finished the discussion, think about a difficulty you have had in your life and write about what you did to overcome that obstacle.

Louis Armstrong was a great jazz musician and singer. He played the trumpet and recorded many albums. Perhaps you have heard his recording of "It's a Wonderful World," the song from the movie "Good Morning, Vietnam." Mr. Armstrong was a much beloved performer, but as a young boy he was neglected and abandoned by his parents. He began playing the horn when he lived at a home for boys.

Winston Churchill was a great world leader who, as Prime Minister of Great Britain, helped defeat Adolf Hitler in World War II. As a young boy in school, however, Mr. Churchill failed his grade, and later he repeatedly failed the test to be admitted to the Military Academy.

Oprah Winfrey is a television and movie celebrity today, but as a child she was abused and as a teenager she was sent to a juvenile detention center. Ms. Winfrey is admired not only for her work on television and in the movies, but for the charitable causes she sponsors and promotes.

Dave Thomas is seen on TV commercials advertising his Wendy's restaurant chain. As a boy, he dropped out of school and worked hard to make it in the fast-food business. Starting at the lowest wages, Mr. Thomas worked his way up to management and after becoming successful with his franchise, went back to school for his high school diploma!

Wilma Rudolph, in the 1960 Olympics, won gold medals in track and field, and became known as "the fastest woman in the world." As a young child, however, Ms. Rudolph was sickly. She had polio and for a while could not walk.

Can you think of other famous people who have overcome difficulty to be successful? Who are they?

What difficulty have you had, and how have you handled this challenge in your life?

____

____

____

____

____

____

____

____

a school counselor about your feelings. Usually, talking about these concerns with someone else will help you get direction and enable you to solve your problems.

In addition to proper eating, exercising, resting, cleaning, grooming, thinking, and behaving, your body requires regular maintenance. This means taking steps to see your physician, dentist, counselor, or other professionals for checkups, vaccinations, and advice about how to maintain your health. It also means following their suggestions about how to care for yourself. Taking medicine as directed, watching your weight, brushing and flossing your teeth, seeking support from friends, and doing other things to ensure that your body and mind are in optimal health are a few ways that you invite yourself.

Maintaining good health relates to all the areas—a healthy diet, proper rest and exercise, bodily care, good grooming, and positive thinking. All of these healthful goals require specific behaviors that you should do for yourself. They also contribute to the goal of making friends.

Gold Nugget

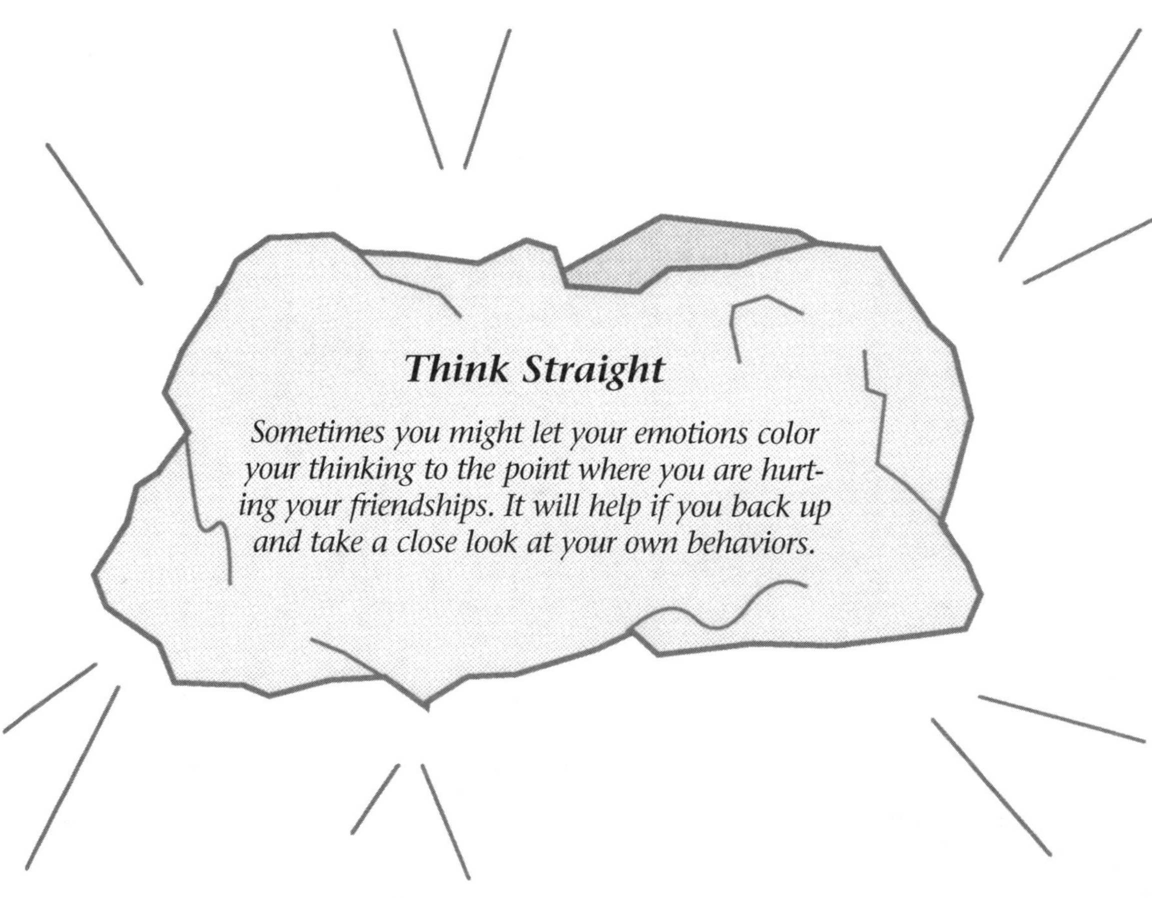

Role Play 9-A
Mirror, Mirror on the Wall

Instructions: Your group leader will ask for volunteers from the class, and explain that the students who volunteer will look at a mirror and talk to it as if they were having a conversation with another person. In this conversation, student volunteers will talk about one thing they would like to change about themselves and explain how they would go about making that change.

As you watch the role play, write down words and phrases you think are important. After each role play, you can discuss with the class what you heard. Look for:

1. Optimistic messages
2. Self-responsibility
3. Courage to change
4. Healthy views of self

MAKING FRIENDS

The purpose of this program is to share some ideas about friendship and how friends can be helpful in your life. It is appropriate to end it with the idea that if you want to enjoy life to its fullest, you will invite yourself to form many friendships. Some of these friendships will be brief and some may be lasting, but all of your friendships will contribute to your life.

As you learned some of the ideas in this program, you might have said to yourself, "That's simple, everyone knows that." Or, maybe you thought, "This is easy, anyone can make friends." True, many of the ideas in this book appear to be easy, and maybe for you they are easy! However, other people may have difficulty with things you think are easy. Remember in Section 6 when you learned about "how to invite," and it was compared to learning how to hit a golf ball? Everyone has different ideas and views about how easy things are. See if you think Activity 9.4 is easy.

How did you do in Activity 9.4 with the Novak Shuffle? If you were not successful on the first try, by all means go back and try again. If you were successful, congratulations! You might want to try it with a group of friends or your family to see if they think it is simple or difficult.

Name ______________________________ Date ________________

ACTIVITY 9.4
The "Novak Shuffle"

A friend of mine uses a demonstration to show how things that sometimes look simple or easy can often be complex or difficult. My friend, Dr. John Novak, is a professor of education at Brock University in Canada. I call his demonstration the "Novak Shuffle." Try it and see if you think it is a good demonstration of how things look simple but are hard for some people. Here is how to do the Novak Shuffle:

First, take your left hand and put it on your nose.

That's right, hold your nose with your left hand.

Next, take your right hand and hold your left ear.

Got it? Okay, that is the simple part.

Now, your group leader will count, and at the count of three you are going to reverse the positions of your hands.

You will put your right hand on your nose and your left hand on your right ear.

Ready? One, Two, Three, Go!

Doing the Novak Shuffle
Cartoon 9-A

Many factors will influence your friendships throughout your life. Most important are the friendly messages that you create and send to yourself and others. The quality, frequency, and duration of the messages you send will directly influence the quality, frequency, and duration of friendships you encounter. If you cultivate trust, respect, and optimism, and you intentionally invite yourself and others frequently, consistently, and dependably, you will increase the likelihood of being successful in your friendships and in your life. Now have fun with Activities 9.5 and 9.6!

One More Invitation

Now that you have taken the time to try this program on friendship, and have completed its lessons, stories, and activities, I would like to hear from you. In particular, I would like to know what you think about this idea of "invitations," and whether you think it is a helpful way to learn about friendship. Any suggestions you have about changing this program to make it better in helping students to learn about friendship are appreciated.

You may write to me at: Dr. John J. Schmidt, P.O. Box 2428, Greenville, NC 27836-0428.

Best wishes in developing and receiving many invitations throughout your life!

Name ______________________ Date ______________

ACTIVITY 9.5
Draw a Nebbish

Throughout this program, you have seen cartoons, which I call "nebbishes." I hope you have enjoyed them. Now draw your own nebbish—one that you would want to be a "best friend."

Name ______________________________ Date ______________

ACTIVITY 9.6
Treat Yourself

Do something nice for yourself. Think about something you have wanted to do for yourself, plan it, and make it happen. Use this activity sheet to write down your plan. If it is something that costs money, figure out ways to earn the money and save for it. The important thing is to do something for yourself every now and then. You deserve it!

Friends
Cartoon 9-B

Appendix A

GROUP LEADER PLANNING GUIDE

Notes
Section 1: Understanding Friendship
Points and themes to emphasize:

____

____

____

____

____

____

____

Supplemental materials:

____

____

____

____

____

____

____

Ideas for using cartoons:

____

____

____

____

____

____

____

Ideas for using Gold Nuggets:

Vocabulary and concepts to explain:

Additional activities, role plays, and assignments:

Section 2: Becoming Friends

Points and themes to emphasize:

Supplemental materials:

Ideas for using cartoons:

Ideas for using Gold Nuggets:

Vocabulary and concepts to explain:

Additional activities, role plays, and assignments:

Section 3: Learning About Invitations

Points and themes to emphasize:

Supplemental materials:

Ideas for using cartoons:

Ideas for using Gold Nuggets:

Vocabulary and concepts to explain:

Additional activities, role plays, and assignments:

Section 4: Four Levels of Encouraging or Discouraging Friendship

Points and themes to emphasize:

Supplemental materials:

Ideas for using cartoons:

Ideas for using Gold Nuggets:

Vocabulary and concepts to explain:

Additional activities, role plays, and assignments:

Section 5: Knowing Yourself

Points and themes to emphasize:

Supplemental materials:

Ideas for using cartoons:

Ideas for using Gold Nuggets:

Vocabulary and concepts to explain:

Additional activities, role plays, and assignments:

Section 6: Creating Invitations to Friendship

Points and themes to emphasize:

Supplemental materials:

Ideas for using cartoons:

Ideas for using Gold Nuggets:

Vocabulary and concepts to explain:

Additional activities, role plays, and assignments:

Section 7: Making Choices and Resolving Differences

Points and themes to emphasize:

Supplemental materials:

Ideas for using cartoons:

Ideas for using Gold Nuggets:

Vocabulary and concepts to explain:

Additional activities, role plays, and assignments:

Section 8: Choosing Positive Behaviors

Points and themes to emphasize:

Supplemental materials:

Ideas for using cartoons:

Ideas for using Gold Nuggets:

Vocabulary and concepts to explain:

Additional activities, role plays, and assignments:

Section 9: Sending Yourself Invitations

Points and themes to emphasize:

Supplemental materials:

Ideas for using cartoons:

Ideas for using Gold Nuggets:

Vocabulary and concepts to explain:

Additional activities, role plays, and assignments:

Appendix B

Bibliography of Invitational Resources

Invitational theory began in the 1970s with William Purkey's book, *Inviting School Success.* Originally called *invitational education,* it focused mainly on student-teacher relationships. Since that time, several works have expanded the theory, and have attempted to apply the theory to a wide range of settings and in different professional relationships. The following list is provided to help you learn more about invitational theory and its applications.

Lehr, J. & Martin, C. (1992). *We're All at Risk: Inviting Learning for Everyone.* Minneapolis, MN: Educational Media Corporation.

Novak, J. M. (1992). *Advancing Invitational Thinking.* San Francisco, CA: Caddo Gap Press.

Purkey, W. W. & Novak, J. M. (1996). *Inviting School Success: A Self-Concept Approach to Teaching,* 3rd ed. Belmont, CA: Wadsworth.

Purkey, W. W. & Novak, J. M. (1988). *Education: By Invitation Only.* Bloomington, IN: Phi Delta Kappa.

Purkey, W. W., & Schmidt, J. J. (1996). *Invitational Counseling: A Self-Concept Approach to Professional Practice.* Pacific Grove, CA: Brooks/Cole.

Purkey, W. W., & Schmidt, J. J. (1990). *Invitational Learning for Counseling and Development.* Ann Arbor, MI: ERIC/CAPS.

Purkey, W. W., & Stanley, P. H. (1991). *Invitational Teaching, Learning, and Living.* Washington, DC: National Education Association.

Purkey, W. W. & Stanley, P. H. (1997). *The Inviting School Treasury: 1,001 Ways to Invite Student Success.* Greenville, NC: Brookcliff Publishers.

Purkey, W. W., & Strahan, D. (1987). *Positive Discipline: A Pocketful of Ideas.* Columbus, OH: National Middle Schools Association.

Schmidt, J. J. (1994). *Living Intentionally & Making Life Happen,* Revised Ed. Greenville, NC: Brookcliff Publishers.

Wilson, J. H. (1986). *The Invitational Elementary Classroom.* Springfield, IL: Charles C. Thomas.

Appendix C

Bibliography of Friendship Books for Students

The books listed in this appendix offer a sample of supplemental guides to friendship and other relationships, as well as books that tell stories about friendships. These instructional guides may provide additional activities and ideas to help students explore their friendships further. The readers will allow students to cover a wide range of issues related to friendship. It is recommended that you read any book prior to assigning it to students. By reading the book yourself, you will be able to assess its appropriateness for your grade level and the topics you wish to address.

Instructional and Self-Help Books

Feelings about Friends by Linda Swartz. 1988. Learning Works. A workbook to help children get in touch with their feelings. Offers help in making friends and resolving conflicts. Grades 3-6.

Friendship and Love by Dale C. Garell. 1989. Chelsea House, New York. Chapters include: The many faces of intimacy; How we learn to love; Our first friendships; Adolescence and Adulthood; Men, women & intimacy; A world of differences.

How to Make and Keep Friends by Elizabeth Karlsberg. 1991. Troll Associates, Mahwah, NJ. A friendship book for girls. Gives helpful hints and advice on getting along with people, grooming, health, dealing with cliques, and patching up arguments, among other topics. Appropriate for grades 7 and 8.

Making Friends, Finding Love: A Book About Teen Relationships by Julie Tallard Johnson. 1992. Lerner Publications, Minneapolis, MN. Offers advice about building friendships and establishing romantic relationships.

Popularity Has Its Ups and Downs by Meg F. Schneider. 1991. Simon & Schuster, New York. A kind of self-help book consisting of the following chapters: Who Wants to Be Popular?; The Great Popularity Myths; Who is the Real You?; You and Mr. or Mrs. Popularity; Friendship—The Only Popularity that Really Counts; Popularity and Romance; The Shyness Factor; How to Handle Being on the "Outs" with the "In" Crowd; Kids Talk about Popularity.

Ready-to-Use Social Skills Lessons & Activities for Grades 7-12 by Ruth Weltmann Begun. 1996. The Center for Applied Research in Education. This manual provides an activity-based curriculum of real-life situations to help students develop self-esteem, increase self-control, demonstrate respectful behavior, and take responsibility for their actions.

Relationships and Communication Activities by Patricia Rizzo Toner. 1993. The Center for Applied Research in Education. An activity guide that includes 90 ready-to-use worksheets for grades 7-12, this book is part of a health curriculum series. It includes activities about family relationships, friendship, dating and marriage, general relationships, skills and methods of communication, group dynamics, and communication breakdown.

Relationships: In and Out of Family by Sharon Carter Rosen, 1987, Discusses the benefits of friendships—how to form and keep them. Volume 2 of *The Young Adult Reader's Adviser.*

The Best Friends Book by Arlene Erlback. 1995. Free Spirit. Real best friends recall what ingredients have enabled them to form lasting friendships. The second part of the book provides activities for friends to do together. For Grades 4-7.

Your Circle of Friends by Claudine G. Wirths and Mary Bowman-Fruhm. 1993. Twenty-first Century Books, New York. An easy-to-read self-help book, appropriate for ages 9-13. Chapters include: Introduction, A Friend Indeed, Making Friends, Keeping a Friend, When a Friend Needs Help, Special Friends, In-Groups and other Groups, and 20 Fun Things to Do with Close Friends. Includes some cartoons.

Friendship Readers

Alan and Naomi by Myron Levoy. 1981. Dell. Story of a girl whose father is killed by soldiers. Alan helps her deal with the loss. Recommended for grades 7-9.

Always and Forever Friends by Carole S. Adler. 1988. Ticknor. About a girl named Wendy who has a difficult time after her friend, Meg, moves away. She meets Honor who is hesitant to accept Wendy's friendship. Grades 5-7.

Bathing Ugly by Rebecca Busselle. 1989. Watts (Orchard Books). Problems with teasing and ruthlessness at summer camp. Grades 6-8.

Bobby and the Brockles Go to School by Adele Faber & Elaine Mazlish. 1994. Avon. Students are mean to their new classmate, Bobby. Then two extraterrestrial visitors arrive and teach Bobby about making friends. Grades 3-5.

Bridge to Terabithia by Katherine Paterson. 1977. Crowell, New York. A Newbery Medal Winner, this book tells the story of Jess, the fastest runner in the 5th grade. A girl named Leslie comes to school and replaces Jess as the fastest runner. In time, they form a friendship that lasts until tragedy strikes. Recommended for grades 5-8.

Come a Stranger by Cynthia Voigt. 1986. Atheneum. About a girl, named Mina, who goes to a summer dance camp and makes friends. Deals with handling differences and rejection in friendship. Recommended for grades 4-7.

Cricket and the Crackerbox Kid by Alane Ferguson. 1990. Bradbury. A story about a girl who adopts a dog at the pound and tribulations that follow. Classroom activity involved to end the story. Grades 5-8.

Fried Green Tomatoes at the Whistle Stop Cafe by Fannie Flagg. 1987. Random House. A beautiful story of two older women and their lasting friendship. Recommended for grades 6 and above.

Friends Forever by Miriam Chaikin. 1988. Harper. A sentimental story that takes place in the war years about Molly and her friends. For grades 4-6.

Hating Alison Ashley by Robin Klein. 1987. Viking. Tells what happens when the bright student in the class is replaced by a new student to school. For grades 5-8.

Hear the Wind Blow by Patricia Pendergraft. 1988. Putnam. Story takes place in a small town and tells about the relationship between a student, Isadora Clay, and the "meanest boy in school." For grades 5-7.

Indian Summer by Barbara Girion. 1993. Scholastic. Story of two girls who resist friendship, but eventually they become great friends. Recommended for grades 4-7.

Just Good Friends by Dean Marney. 1982. Harper. About Lou, a thirteen-year-old who forms a friendship with two men as he learns to deal with adolescence. Grades 5-8.

Just Like Jenny by Sandy Asher. 1982. Delacorte. About the friendship of two girls and the ballet classes. Recommended for grades 5-8.

Lizzie Logan Wears Purple Sunglasses by Eileen Spinelli. 1994. Simon and Schuster. A funny book about two girls named Heather and Lizzie. Recommended for grades 3-5.

Queen of the Sixth Grade by Ilene Cooper. 1988. Morrow. Story of competition for leadership and about being an outsider. Grades 4-6.

Ronnie and Rosey by Judie Angell. 1977. Dell. Ronnie, a girl, and Rosey, a boy, form a close friendship after the death of Ronnie's father. Grades 5-7.

Take a Chance Gramps by Joy Davies Okimoto. 1990. Little, Brown and Co. A story about youth and its relationship to older people. Grades 7-8.

The Buffalo Nickel Blues Band by Judie Angell. 1982. Bradbury. A story about five kids who form a band. Grades 5-8.

The Fourth Grade Dinosaur Club by Larry Bograd. 1989. Delacorte. Story of Billy and his Hispanic friend, Juan. For grades 4-6.

The Magic of the Glits by Carole S. Adler. 1987. Avon. This book is about a twelve-year-old boy named Jeremy who takes care of a seven-year-old girl for the summer. Grades 5-7.

The Twits by Roald Dahl. 1981. Random House. A zany story about friends who drive each other crazy. Recommended for grades 6-8.

They're All Named Wildfire by Nancy Springer. 1989. Macmillan. Story of two friends who share a love for horses. Recommended for grades 4-6.

Tina Gogo by Judie Angell. 1980. Dell. Story of a girl who becomes friends with another girl who is unusual and irresponsible. Grades 5-8.

Today Fifth Grade Tomorrow the World by Candice F. Ransom. 1989. Willowisp Press. Tells about trying too hard to be part of the "in group." Grades 5-8.

What's the Opposite of a Best Friend? by Auline Bates. 1991. Scholastic. About two best friends and their differences. Grades 4-8.

Where the Sidewalk Ends by Shel Silverstein. 1974. Harper and Row. A book of humorous poetry about friendship by a popular children's poet. Book for young children, but enjoyed by all ages.

Whose Side Are You On? by Emily Moore. 1988. Farrar, Straus and Giroux. Looks at different aspects of friendship, particularly its uncertainty. Grades 7-8.

Yellow Bird & Me by Joyce Hansen. 1986. Ticknor. Story of differences and friendship. Grade 4-6.